In this world, the simply constant is "change". – which is a massive challenge in the world of Business. One notable event is the world-altering outbreak of the COVID-19, which significantly made a considerable impact in all businesses all over the globe, no exemptions. With this business climate, the world is experiencing, what future awaits every person in business in 2021? Will still there be businessmen with brave hearts to take some risks all over again? What enterprises can we consider starting up in the COVID aftermath? – ever sensation what it takes to be a resilient businessman? Congratulations! You're on your way of finding out after reading this book.

"THE RESILIENT ENTERPRISES"
Most Challenging 2021

MEVIN MCDONALD

"THE RESILIENT ENTERPRISES"

Most Challenging 2021

Copyright © 2020 by **G A B M S M WICKRAMASINGHE**

All rights reserved. No part of this book may be reproduced or used in any manner without written permission of the copyright owner (Author) except for the use of quotations in a book review. For more information, email address: mevinmcdonald@gmail.com

THE FACT THAT AN ORGANIZATION OR WEBSITE IS REFERRED TO IN THIS WORK AS A CITATION AND/OR A POTENTIAL SOURCE OF FURTHER INFORMATION DOES NOT MEAN THAT THE AUTHOR ENDORSES THE INFORMATION THE ORGANIZATION OR WEBSITE MAY PROVIDE OR RECOMMENDATIONS IT MAY MAKE. FURTHER, READERS SHOULD BE AWARE THAT INTERNET WEBSITES LISTED IN THIS WORK MAY HAVE CHANGED OR DISAPPEARED BETWEEN WHEN THIS WORK WAS WRITTEN AND WHEN IT IS READ

FIRST EDITION | Dec-2020

"The Resilient Enterprises"

"THE RESILIENT ENTERPRISES"

Most Challenging 2021

About the Author

I'm an optimistic guy – yes, that's me. Being happy does not mean I never think negatively; it only means I always choose to think of good thoughts over not so lovely ideas, but that's how I programmed my mindset. Some would call me sophisticated; perhaps at some point, I am.

Well, here's how I grew up. I Raised in a middle-class family. I was fortunate to finish my education successfully. But, 'successful' means reaching my high school final year and having good grades. But that doesn't mean I did well in school. The real score behind it was when I was a child. I like going to school to play and avoid periods with my classmates at school. That's what excites me the most, and not the studies. That's how we spend time mostly at school.

A week after my high school advanced level examination, I joined a telecommunications company as a salesman. I stared at my career and looked at myself as a sales guy, it wasn't an easy task, I look too young, it's even difficult to convince people, no one is willing to buy what I sell them, but that didn't stop me giving up wasn't an option. I had to move forward amidst frustrations and focus on my failures; despite difficulties, I had to move on; it's the only option I have. I don't have sufficient funds, I need to work hard, and the only investment I had with me then was self-trust. I cannot leave this game; instead, I concentrated myself to expect failures and learn from mistakes. During the time of this most challenging decade, I have worked in telecommunication, FMCG Fast-moving Consumer Goods, Banking, Information Technology, Airline, International Education, and Business Data Solutions

"THE RESILIENT ENTERPRISES"

Most Challenging 2021

industries, as well. These experiences gave me so much systematic work culture exposure in different fields, both local and international.

Meanwhile, I completed my Bachelor's degree in Business Administration and my Master's degree in Science of Strategic Marketing while doing hard work. During these consecutive sales-oriented years, I conducted self-motivation programs, suicide prevention programs, business consultations, and everything I could to keep the human brain the positive way I did. Apart from that, I did a lot of research, as well. By that time, one of the best analysis I ever did for mobile germs and bacteria during my spare time. I was even able to invent a herbal liquid cleanser, which can be used for mobile phone cleaning on the exterior surfaces. After 60 Months of Dedicated hard work, I have obtained a patent license as well. Henceforth Apart from my professional corporate life, I would say I'm a well-planned resilient businessman, I can see my well-developed invention surpassed my corporate income, and it did! I want to thank these two significant Australians who invested in my innovation. And, as the COVID-19 pandemic slapped us with a reality that nothing is constant but change. Thus, this made me decide to share my knowledge. This book is not about my personal life, but this is how I technically realize how can reach money for the betterment of humans and everything in between. This book will teach you how 'resiliency' wins in almost every situation. From experience, it would be my pleasure to share what an entrepreneur should know to win this 'fluctuating situation' game as what this pandemic caused the whole economy.

"THE RESILIENT ENTERPRISES"

Most Challenging 2021

Table of Contents

About the Author 3
    What a challenge for 2021! 8
Chapter 2 "Business in the 'New Normal – Survival from the global pandemic." 11
    Adapt to the Unusual 13
    The Rise of the Digital Economy 14
Chapter 3 "A Resilient Businessman" 16
    Stand still in the Face of Catastrophe 18
    Aim to Fail 19
    A resilient Businessman is a Vision-driven Entrepreneur 21
Chapter 4 "Masters of the digital age" 23
Chapter 5 "The Business Start-up Grind" 29
    Identify your exclusive selling option: 30
    Direct distribution 65
    Retail distribution 65
    Milestones and Metrics 66
    Company Overview and Team 68
    Mission Statement 71
    Financial Plan 71
    Sales or Income or Revenue 74
    Interest, Taxes, Depreciation, and Repayment 75
Chapter 6 "The Business Start-up Essentials" 90
    Business Planning 90
    Market Analysis 91

"THE RESILIENT ENTERPRISES"
Most Challenging 2021

- Capital Investment 92
- Marketing 93
- The Marketing Strategies 94
- The Marketing Concepts 97
- The 7P formula of Marketing 99
- Branding 105
- Maintaining Brand Personality 106
- The Big Five Personality Traits 108

Chapter 7 "Sales Master" 113
- Basics of a Seller 113
- The Art of Persuasion 116

Chapter 8 "Mevin's Consumer's Grade Approach" 121
- Vigilance – the Secret Weapon 124

Chapter 9 "Shaping up a Business-oriented mindset" 126
- The Law of Attraction 131

Chapter 10 "Another 20 years of Resilient Businesses" 132
- Nanosatellite 139
- Business Process Outsourcing 143
- Web Designing 144
- Search Engine Optimization (SEO) 146
- Management organizations 148
- Research / Observations / conclusions / citations and related theories 153

"THE RESILIENT ENTERPRISES"

Most Challenging 2021

Chapter 1

Introduction

In a world full of uncertainty, resiliency is a MUST for an entrepreneur to survive in the business world. Not only will it save you from the darkness of the unknown, but it will also prepare you to combat the constantly changing market where only those who can effectively foresee what lies ahead can step their business forward. Suppose you do not know, discovery out more about being a resilient businessman. Learn more about how resilient a business person should be to reign over the challenges the world is randomly giving, like this catastrophic pandemic from which we are all suffering and struggling.

In this world, the simple constant is "change". – Which is a massive challenge in the world of business. One notable event is the world-altering outbreak of the COVID-19, which remarkably made an enormous impact on all industries all over the globe, with no exemptions. With this business climate, the world is experiencing, what future awaits every person in business in 2021? Will there still be businessmen with brave hearts to take some risks all over again? Which enterprise can we consider starting up in the COVID aftermath? – Ever sensation what it takes to be a resilient businessman? Congratulations! You're on your way to finding out after reading this book. This book will teach you the qualities a resilient entrepreneur should have to survive this journey towards the unknown.

"THE RESILIENT ENTERPRISES"

Most Challenging 2021

It is crucial that before you decide to take the path of entrepreneurship, conceptual imagination is the first thing you know, and when it's come to the commercial level of how the system of the business works. Make sure you equip yourself with what is fully necessary, especially now that industry is becoming riskier as different generations pass.

What a challenge for 2021!

2021 will be the most challenging year of this decade.

The beginning of 2020 went fine; people were able to celebrate Valentines in February even with a face mask on, coffee shops, cafes can see everywhere, which means retailers were still doing fine, at least. March came outbreaks everywhere in the world. Were forced All business establishments to shut down with no exemptions. Big or small, companies have to close per government health protocols. As a result, the economy drowned. All investments globally were at stake. No one had foreseen it, not even Jack Ma, the great businessman of his time, saw it coming. Some business owners tried several times to recover from their loss. While COVID seemed to lay low at some point, in some areas, the government declared allowing the reopening of selected business industries that were previously ordered closed, helping recover their losses, and at least saving those on the verge of bankruptcy. Some companies did try their best. Manufacturing companies suffered the hardest. For some, the best they can do is offer employees an option to work from home.

They did! Almost all companies resorted to working remotely, in a desperate hope that everything's going to be good gradually. Unfortunately, again, the second wave, the third wave came. Governments declared lockdown all over again.

"THE RESILIENT ENTERPRISES"

Most Challenging 2021

"Until when?" – The only question left in my mind was this: how can expect economy regaining? When is the outbreak recurring? The worst part is that it is unknown when it will strike again. Above all, it is unknown until when should we expect it to be like that.

These situations made 90% of businesses worldwide stuck in the middle of the unknown; none of these businesses generates revenue, instead of incurring expenses. How unfortunate. With a small staff, companies still find it hard to pay their salaries as there were no profits earned during these times, as the virus persistently emerged. With this considerable loss, every business person in the world suffered too – no revenue, no profit, bankruptcy threats are everywhere, and it will probably be so until the end of the year. How are people in business supposed to start in 2021? What will the source of the fund be if companies continuously suffer from incurring expenses without any revenue? It's perhaps the most challenging question to answer this time. A sad truth that we should have accepted for long, "change is constant" – this tragic reality will leave you hanging with a sad thought: 'Will I still build up my own business in 2021?' It is undeniable that this sudden virus outbreak pained our economy hard in every corner of the world. At some point, it will indeed hold us up and just let go of the idea of starting a business. For most people, this will be the expected thought. But for resilient men, that's not going to be the case. A resilient businessman will always think, 'There will always be a way out.' We will talk about it better in the next chapter, 'what it takes to be a resilient businessman, and how being one will prepare you to battle against these kinds of inevitable events that leave a significant impact on the world of business.

"THE RESILIENT ENTERPRISES"

Most Challenging 2021

So, while our current situation would say, "Never start a business in 2021," every resilient businessman would reply, "why wouldn't I when there are some routes to take?"

As COVID continuously challenged the world's economy, everyone sought some ways out. On average, everyone resorted to technology; were introduced remote workers in the corporate world. Working from home has been offered to employees in most companies. While it is the only option to take, no employees would still dare report to the office. Thus, work from home has become effective. As useful as it was very convenient for them. Needless to say that Technology-based businesses are the ones making excellent business survival nowadays, which is precisely the content of our next chapter. – Business in the 'new normal.' So, do you still doubt whether you should start a business in 2021? The answer is yes; you still can, and, above all, you should! 'Technology' simply answers "HOW" of starting up a business all over again in the COVID aftermath in 2021. Let's talk more about it in the next chapter.

"THE RESILIENT ENTERPRISES"

Most Challenging 2021

Chapter 2

"Business in the 'New Normal – Survival from the global pandemic."

Over the past decade, technology and internet use were factors in the significant growth many businesses experienced. According to the long-term plan, most multi-billion companies invested billions of money to the following:

1. Technology innovation
2. Infrastructure
3. Science
4. Education etc.

2020 came, COVID-19 sudden outbreak emerged all over the globe. Everyone started working from home to cope with the crisis. As a result, the use of technology in doing business rose to overcome this climate; every industry worldwide is experiencing. So, to ensure survival in these trying times, almost all companies in different sectors started developing comprehensive digital presences. Although fostered technology innovation was before the onset of the economy-stopping business climate we are experiencing. It predicted that remote works would make their way up for the next decades, more or less. Now, the COVID-19 pandemic is making it realized. Just with the short-term effect, every business owner felt changes that will rise. An estimated 75% of teams worldwide were foreseen to be doing remote works in the

"THE RESILIENT ENTERPRISES"
Most Challenging 2021

coming years. Although, to some extent, depending on every business's engagements, face to face work is still going to be needed, which is the most expected major cultural shifts in the world of business for the next decade. Which, in most cases, are going to be advantageous for both employees and employers in the following areas:

1. It means high potential salary savings for employees, as they won't be spending commuting to their respective offices. Thus, many would get interested in working for your business. As such, it will be some enhancement in workforces to all companies worldwide. Moreover, since working from home is undeniably more convenient for every employee, such convenience would also increase employee productivity, which is an excellent advantage on the employer's part.
2. As a result of these positive impacts of work-from-home trend sudden shift in the business environment, it could mean happiness to every employee. We know for a fact that a happy employee means an efficient, effective, and productive employee. And a productive employee also means a satisfied employer. If this cycle goes, it could lead to a successful business, just by merely looking at the brighter side of these global pandemic effects to the business world more than just looking at the opposing side.

We may be drowning amidst these so-called tough economic times. But, practically speaking, this so-called "new normal," as they call it, only requires a proper mindset for every businessman. Focusing on the bad will only worsen things. Instead, be more professional enough in dealing with this catastrophic shift in the world of business. In the next chapter,

"THE RESILIENT ENTERPRISES"

Most Challenging 2021

we'll be discussing more being a resilient businessman. But let us talk more about adapting to the unusual in this chapter's subtopic. Keep going.

Adapt to the Unusual

As the 'new normal' thing kissed the economy 'hello,' leaving it with no choice but to deal with it, all businessmen are still totally spooked by the exceptionally unusual situation prompting us. How are each one expected to adapt to this unique situation? Will the recently just starting up businesses manage?

Almost all of us got used face to face interactions with colleagues at work. And, businessmen perhaps are used to meeting with the clients on official business trips. Almost all companies serve customers face-to-face, saving those already exposed in the digital world. Everyone in the pre-COVID was productive in their everyday lives at work. Unfortunately, this pandemic can't be an excuse not to be productive. Having to stay effective fighting through this worst time of this decade's toughest epidemic is challenging and frightening. Who would choose the economy over health? No one, for sure.

These must be a wake-up call to every entrepreneur on "preparedness." How prepared is your business for what's coming? – having slapped with a huge climate, every business person should develop contingency plans to ensure preparedness in facing situations such as what we have now. As an entrepreneur, you must always revisit your entire business model to see what changes or improvements are required to ensure your business is ready for what's coming up.

"THE RESILIENT ENTERPRISES"

Most Challenging 2021

In the next chapter, we'll talk more about how the digital economy takes its turn in the market now.

The Rise of the Digital Economy

While the average economy is struggling amidst COVID, the digital economy is thriving. Must be a reality check for businesses that have been reluctant to embrace the digital transformation and now find themselves woefully unprepared after COVID-19 struck the whole world with disgust. And, as the pandemic continues to scare the potentially health-compromised employees, business owners are now scrambling and cramming to migrate their operations and workforce to a virtual environment. This sudden transformation was quick due to the immediate lockdown protocol across the globe, which isn't only a wake-up call and a profound realization of how vital internet access and the digital economy play during crises and now. Suppose there are still some doubts lingering around you on the silver lining of the digital economy's rise. In that case, the following are what you should consider when putting up your own business, putting the spotlight on the digital-based company's advantages.

Start Digitization now!

The digital economy is currently making, following are the reasons why business digitization is essential:

- **Productivity:**

Firms that embraced digital solutions even before COVID-19 are ready to work remotely. So, they focus on leveraging collaboration and tools to maximize workforce productivity and sustain company culture. Thus, making its business functions more productive than what it does in the average economy, making them the most prepared firms to combat the crisis and still operate with consistent productivity than other businesses do.

- **Efficiency:**

While it is undeniable that technology-based processes work faster than the usual manual processes do. The digital economy stands out now than ever as compared to what businesses did in the regular economy. Needless to say that even without a climate such as the pandemic we are currently experiencing, digital-based firms are still ideal when talking about efficiency.

"THE RESILIENT ENTERPRISES"

Most Challenging 2021

Chapter 3

"A Resilient Businessman"

What do you think does it take to be a resilient businessman? And, how does being one prepares you to combat the unknown? Will it save you in this kind of pandemic we are all suffering? – An uncertain event for all of us all these times.

Talking about how a business can survive by developing comprehensive digital presences or merely enhancing the use of technology in the industry in the previous chapter, we will now speak on how resilient can save you and your business during trying times COVID-19, which we all didn't expect. So, let's start with the question: "Is it enough that you know all the basic in starting up a business, then you can go?" "In starting up a business, how relevant it is to prepare yourself to be a resilient businessman, if not the great one?

So, when can we say a businessman is resilient? Talk about resilience; a resilient business person can identify emerging threats and clearly understands possible impacts of these to the business as a whole. On a more detailed discussion, the following are the qualities every resilient business person has, and here are some discussions on how helpful it is for them as businessmen:

First, a resilient businessman is one who is innovative at all costs in any situation. Not only will being innovative can save you in whatever crisis that will strike anytime to crash your

"THE RESILIENT ENTERPRISES"

Most Challenging 2021

business down. It also increases the chances for your business to grow and succeed no matter what, at any circumstance, and under whatever business climate, it is the heart of the company, as they said. Being innovative can also lead you to create more efficient processes in doing your business that may result in better and advanced productivity and performance. A very creative business owner indeed owns those surviving businesses amidst this pandemic.

Secondly, a resilient businessman is one who keeps himself always up to fast-paced technology development. – This is perhaps the most important one. Which was discussed in the previous chapter that action every business person has to do to ensure survival amidst the COVID-19 pandemic is to start developing a comprehensive digital presence, which means to enhance technology-based business processes. One way to achieve that is to keep yourself up about the trend in technology development in all areas. One example we may note is the sudden outbreak of COVID-19 again. When the attack became worst, and everyone started working, it was difficult for some employees to perform their tasks due to limited personal interactions between subordinates and supervisors. But for those who are well-versed in digital platforms, it is normal for them to change from face to face interaction to virtual meetings because they are used to interacting most of the time through digital communication platforms. This made zoom the most used online application by most advanced companies throughout our battle against the COVID crisis.

Lastly, a resilient businessman is a vigilant one in today's globally-connected business world. A businessman needs to be as sharp as ever to be prepared to handle every challenge that the business might face along the way, and that sums up the entirety of what is a resilient businessman as a whole.

In conclusion, it's never enough that you venture into a business that you think is resilient; no! You also have to be resilient yourself being a businessman. Apart from those mentioned above, a real resilient businessman is both an optimist and a pessimist altogether, one who always thinks about the chances of meeting issues as they go along in the business, one who still considers that market fluctuations and business disasters are inevitable. Being a resilient businessman who would always look at both sides of each coin, he would also prepare his business model very sensitively and systematically to cope with the uncertainties. Talking with industry professionals is also one necessary business preparation for every resilient business person do. It is essential to say that business consultants are more conversant about predictive analytical knowledge to optimize what lies ahead. They see the future as more advanced when an industry professional makes financial allocations, enabling them to foresee possible calamity in all business areas.

Stand still in the Face of Catastrophe

A resilient businessman is one who remains even in the face of Catastrophe. – It means not being moved easily by serious threats the business is facing. Indeed, starting a business is like a never-ending path of setbacks, challenges, and potential roadblocks from start to finish. The climate may be inevitable, but the way you design your setbacks is entirely up to your creativity, which might help you succeed.

"THE RESILIENT ENTERPRISES"

Most Challenging 2021

Have it noted that the only difference between failure and success in business is simply answerable by the question **"Who's willing to stick with what he started the smartest way?"** – it doesn't mean you have to be the smartest, not even what talent you have nor skills. It's merely **'resilience.'** In reality, no amount of educational attainment beats resilience. The total score is, those with strong resiliency often have an easier time facing challenges; the same holds in business. Simply because they'll be less likely to give up easily when prompted with difficulties; instead, they'll be steadfast and unwavering. They'll instead find facing obstacles as a way to find actionable solutions more quickly because they're not trying to avoid or ignore any unpleasant facts before them. Instead, they face it and find concrete solutions for their struggles.

Aim to Fail

While it is mainstream to every human being, business person or not, to avoid failure, resiliency suggests actively seeking for it, instead. Find out why.

Be reminded that **'FAIL'** just simply means **F**irst **A**ttempt **i**n **L**earning. – Which means to fail is only one of the ingredients of success, We learn to succeed. And, there are just things learned through failures. Thus, to fail should not be something to avoid being a resilient businessman. Aim for it, instead. A resilient businessman isn't afraid to die because he sees it as an opportunity to grow. Every failure an entrepreneur encounters is a lesson. It is merely a learning experience to help them ensure success on the next attempt. After accepting and learning from those failures, the next effort enables them to

"THE RESILIENT ENTERPRISES"
Most Challenging 2021

step toward success. While all of us want success, let us also consider that committing failures is fine. When you fail, move forward. Don't let yourself be consumed by it. Be always reminded that sometimes, if not most of the time, things aren't going to be as planned, and that's entirely all right. Don't overthink. Failing doesn't in any way invalidates your idea, nor saying your dreams aren't good enough. Instead, it means there is something ahead to be learned about, or there is a better direction to be taken, as FAIL means the first attempt at learning. Hence, there isn't a point to be afraid of failing. It isn't fatal. It's okay. Failure is only there to pause you for a moment to say; there is another shot for you to try it all over again to give you a better outcome. See it like that.

To give you more about it, here are some reasons why failure is equivalent to success on the other side of the coin:

1. **It's a redirection in disguise**: whenever you fail, don't feel bad, be genuinely grateful about it instead. It speaks that you shouldn't be there where you are now. Such failure is a cue for you to proceed differently instead, which has a more fantastic victory waiting for you than what you have in mind.
2. **It's an opportunity to be better**: it's a chance for you to re-evaluate everything after such failure you stumbled into, which impliedly says you can do better, better than what you think you can. It's a chance for you to bounce back and come stronger and with better understanding and reasoning – an opportunity rarely appreciated by many.
3. **Failure is not lethal**: no matter how hard your loss, know that it will never be fatal. It reserves merely another shot for you to it all over again, re-evaluates

"THE RESILIENT ENTERPRISES"

Most Challenging 2021

everything, re-assess yourself, and a chance to give your best try on the next attempt.

A resilient Businessman is a Vision-driven Entrepreneur

Merriam-Webster defines vision as "the ability to see: sight or eyesight, something that you imagine, a picture that you see in your mind, something that you see or dream." Wikipedia gives a more straightforward definition: "Vision is foresight- the capacity to envisage future market trends, and plan accordingly."

In entrepreneurship, a vision has a different meaning. It is way deeper. – it is the vital energy that drives every entrepreneur. Passion is the real driver in almost everything we do; vision is what drives passion too. And, the domino effect goes. Image is what makes a resilient businessman dare. – dare to risk, dare to go beyond, dare to explore more, dare to keep pushing, dare to have the determination to insist and seek success. It represents the frame where the picture of culture lies. It creates and establishes culture, which is the critical component that gets things easy, following a shared norm, expectations, and duties that define organization acts. Some of the great entrepreneurs have achieved their goals by setting a firm, clear, and healthy vision. Mark Zuckerberg of Facebook envisioned Facebook as the community platform to keep people around the world stay connected. A venture's success is about defining and pursuing a vision and being able to formulate it into something tangible and instrument the idea. When the process spread across the organization, it translates into the so-called culture. And that drives everyone to pursue the same path towards success altogether. Thus, vision is the sole key element that helps the entrepreneur through the ups and downs and funnels; Should share its passion perseverance and persistence towards reaching the end goal with the entire organization. Now, let us try to talk more about why it is crucial to be a vision-driven entrepreneur.

First, a vision-driven entrepreneur has an exact focal point for goal-setting and business planning. It means you have that sense of purpose and a clear direction towards achieving your business' goals. Further suggests that you have a defined long-term and short-term goals for your business, which serve as your guide in making decisions along the way.

"THE RESILIENT ENTERPRISES"

Most Challenging 2021

Chapter 4

"Masters of the digital age."

Now that we have subscribed to the digital age already, which was made more intense by the sudden breakout of COVID-19, let us look a little back and talk in this chapter about the people behind some famous, successful digital-based enterprises.

As a refresher, here are some questions to give you clues on who are these people behind the fame the digital world engraved in the business world over the past years. So, how much do you know about Alibaba? Perhaps, at least, you know more about Facebook, as it's part of your daily living. How about Microsoft? You use it most often at work. Now, who do you think are the people behind these digital-based companies who made immense popularity worldwide for the past decades? And, who are still conquering up to the present times despite this global pandemic? The question, did people stopped using Facebook after the COVID-19 outbreak? The answer is no. in fact, this platform's use has been boosted more dramatically by the stay-home health protocol. How about Alibaba? Do you think their sales declined because of COVID-19? The answer is again, no! Instead; it was boosting perhaps, ten times. Why? Because, when China manufactured and supplied massive facemasks, face shields, and alcohol, Alibaba has been the easiest way to source out these essentials to fight COVID, which at some point became locally unavailable to almost every part of the world. Meaning to say, while the

"THE RESILIENT ENTERPRISES"
Most Challenging 2021

pandemic appeared to be a massive threat to other company's economic growth, for Alibaba, it wasn't the case. It became their breakthrough instead. It paved the way for Alibaba to serve almost all countries in different parts of the world with the most in-demand essentials during these times.

Now, let us talk about the big men behind the fame of the digital age.

Here's an interesting fact to start with, did you know that most of these successful men are college dropouts? Let's find out more:

Let us start with **Bill Gates**, sounds familiar? Bill Gates was one of the richest men in the whole world, yes he is! Bill Gates is the founder of the world's largest software business, Microsoft. According to his biography, Gates enrolled at Harvard University in the fall of 1973, originally thinking of pursuing a career in law. Unfortunately, to his parents' dismay, Gates dropped out of college in 1975 to pursue his business, Microsoft, with partner Allen.

Back then, Gates would rather spend more of his time in the computer lab than in class. He did not have a study regimen even unlike the typical university students do; instead, he would get by on a few hours of sleep, be crammed for a test, and still passed with a good grade. His education wasn't that good. As clearly noted, he was a Harvard dropout yet made it to the billionaire club at 31, making him one of the youngest billionaires at 31. with an impressive record of being the world's richest man for 13 long years due to his decision to pursue his tech entrepreneurship passion, which paved the way for him to the top.

"THE RESILIENT ENTERPRISES"
Most Challenging 2021

And, why do you think Microsoft is so successful over the years? It knew that Microsoft is resilient in dealing with its technology-based business for the past decades of doing it. Microsoft Company is smart. They had resources that allowed them to endure many failures without losing their relevance or ability to compete when the market changes. They were late to realize the usefulness of the internet. They hold to the "Windows or nothing" attitude for too long. They have enjoyed great successes with their flagship operating system (Windows), Microsoft Office, enterprise platforms, and many others. Albeit the reigning popularity amongst businesses of the same industry, Microsoft had suffered many failures too. Though most of them were less visible to the public, as with any other company, not everything they do was a success.

Bill Gates is just one; there are still more. How about talking about Jack Ma? This Chinese business, as they said, is indeed a true rags-to-riches story. As stated in his biography, Ma grew up poor in communist China, failed his university entrance exams twice, and got rejected from dozens of job applications, including one at KFC. Before finding success with his third digital-based company, Ma was skinny and often fought with his classmates.

Although Ma made a massive break in the digital world, he was honest enough to admit, "I'm not good at technology" – he even added, "It's a funny thing. I'm running one of China's biggest companies, maybe in the world, but I know nothing about computers. All I know about computers is to send and receive emails and browse." As far as Ma was concerned, even technological knowledge was not necessary to achieve exceptional success as an internet entrepreneur.

"THE RESILIENT ENTERPRISES"
Most Challenging 2021

However, Jack Ma was always open to new ideas. "From day one," he explained in 2004, "all entrepreneurs know that their day is about dealing with difficulty and failure rather than defined by 'success.' My most challenging time hasn't come yet, but it surely will. Nearly a decade of entrepreneurial experience tells me these difficult times can't be evaded or shouldered by others—the entrepreneur must be able to face failure and never give up." – which is what resiliency is.

See what's familiar to these two successful men in the digital era? Both of them are resilient businessmen. Let's check more other big names behind 'resiliency.'

Guess Who's Next.

If you don't know this person, you are seriously out of age. You may not be using some other social networking platform that much, but you don't have an excuse not knowing Facebook. And the brain behind this indispensable social networking platform nowadays is none other than Mark Zuckerberg himself, the name that made the entire world significantly hooked to it, including you. Like Bill Gates, Mark Zuckerberg was also a university drop out. Yet, as reported, he made a record of being the youngest billionaire on the planet who created the remarkably becoming part of everybody's daily lives, Facebook that now has over 1 billion monthly active users.

Because of this platform, people worldwide can quickly and actively keep connecting with their loved ones. Thanks to Mark Zuckerberg. In an article, Zuckerberg talked about the three key factors behind Facebook's success. Learn about them below:

"THE RESILIENT ENTERPRISES"

Most Challenging 2021

Risk-taking: he mentioned risk-taking as one of the driving forces of his business. It was because of its risk-taking attitude that News Feed became one of the core components of its product, he said. It has long been establishing that risk-taking is a necessary and sometimes an uncertain part of success in starting up a business. Needless to mention that every business is indeed fundamentally linked to risk-taking, big or small.

Employees: then he added employees, saying, "What makes a company great are its people, and the critical treason why great talents joined Facebook was that it allowed them to create a leverage impact." For the record, there are about 1,600 engineers on Facebook, managing over 500 million users. Do the math; that's equivalent to one engineer managing over 300,000 users.

Another notable success booster of Facebook is Zuckerberg's vision to make the world better connected. While it seems like nothing can kick Facebook off track, still, there were some worth noting challenges Zuckerberg encountered along with his business. One of Facebook's biggest problems is the recently enacted General Data Protection Regulation (GDPR) in the EU. The new rules took effect in May. Facebook and all other businesses with a digital presence in Europe had to issue new privacy policies to its users and make significant changes to its operations. With this, Facebook (and all others of the like business) had to return to European users and ask for permission to use their data for things like targeted advertisements. These regulations set limits on what data companies can collect and how they can use it, which negatively impacted Facebook's ability to target ads effectively, potentially reducing its pricing power. At the onset, Zuckerberg knew that his start-up would have to overcome

"THE RESILIENT ENTERPRISES"

Most Challenging 2021

considerable obstacles in this kind of venture. But that predicted business threats for Facebook didn't stop him anyway. It is less known for many how many challenges Facebook has to go through. Yet look at Facebook now; you do the critic. Facebook is undeniably reigning over all digital-based business of its kind. That is what 'resiliency' is.

Bill Gates, Jack Ma, Mark Zuckerberg, possessed the qualities of being a resilient businessman; needless to say, it is indeed one of the crucial factors to consider if you wish to see your business on top like them.

We have mentioned a few big men behind successful digital-based enterprises already. Yet, there's still more. And, we can't move forward without him. What model of iPhone do you use? Have you got a clue now? Yes, you guessed it right. I'm talking about Steve Jobs. So, let's talk about him. If you are an iPhone user then, you know him very well. From his humble vision of "computer for the rest of us," Jobs managed to make his way up to the top, making Apple ranked #1 on the Top 100 digital companies worldwide, way ahead of the popular digital-based platforms Facebook and Alibaba. They are only ranked #10 and #11, respectively. And, like his co-brainy men, Jobs was also a college drop out. That doesn't mean you should drop out of your university now; it won't guarantee your success, though, as it's a case to case basis. But, being a resilient businessman will.

"THE RESILIENT ENTERPRISES"

Most Challenging 2021

Chapter 5

"The Business Start-up Grind"

As the famous saying … "the beginning is always the hardest" – the same holds in business. Starting a business will never be as easy as 1-2-3. It takes a lot of courage to decide to pursue a particular venture. It's not like deciding to go on a movie date out of nowhere and just randomly pick which movie you'd like to watch when you get to the cinema. Should be the movie experience more exciting by planning first which day to go perfectly. Above all, check on what movie is currently on hit. In starting a business, it's also the same. It's not enough that you have all the urge to start a business then you go. No! You should do all planning, and you should consider a lot of factors before beginning. All companies begin with conceptual imagination, and we call it an idea. But you will need more than an idea to make your business dream comes to reality. Planning, self-skills, necessary resources, time, management, and a chance of luck – are all critical. I have prepared a checklist containing the fifteen (15) key factors in starting up a business on a more detailed discussion.

This list will surely guide you from the beginning of your business. Keep this as an initial plan; then, you may start your business.

Get your new business running with our 15-step checklist:

"THE RESILIENT ENTERPRISES"

Most Challenging 2021

Identify your exclusive selling option:

This, I can say, is the most important thing to consider before anything else. Starting a business is also like choosing a course to take when entering the university. In business, it's identifying your exclusive selling. And, to make sure you pick the best one, go back to yourself. Do note that every successful endeavour starts with you. Just as you spell 'success,' you can never spell it correctly without "U," right? – That's precisely the point here. In business, just like choosing a course to pursue in college, check on your interests again. What are the things you want to pursue that you are very passionate about What is that something you love doing while enjoying at the same time? But be careful not to be too emotionally-driven. Make sure to align it with your ultimate goals as well. Because basically. Your intention and emotion are two different factors. Simply say you were able to identify what you are very passionate about, ask yourself again, are you willing to do that always for the next five years? If yes, good for you. Then, that's your perfect selling option. If not, go back to the inner self and revisit what makes you happy, which you think can transform into a business.

You need to carry a standard process when you want to start a business, which may determine your success or failure.

New entrepreneurs get excited when they figured out the possibilities of the idea in their imagination that they think about it to the point of living with such a lively floor for a while until all the technical considerations tend to be disregard due to passionately looking forward to it.

"THE RESILIENT ENTERPRISES"
Most Challenging 2021

Of course, the good thing is, sometimes, the idea works anyway despite the lack of the necessary market research. Unfortunately, most of the time, it does not. Worst is, the idea crashes into pieces resulting in uncertainty in its tracks. It would be best if you avoid the latter, and we'll surely help you with that.

The how-to on researching your business idea is just what you need to keep your business goals on track.

- **The Idea Stage**

For some entrepreneurs, getting the idea and looking forward to the possibilities come easy. Yet, doing market research doesn't. – if you are one, this is a red flag for you. Say, if you can outline the size of a multibillion-dollar market but can't even clearly articulate a plan on how to put these ideas into action in the marketplace, it's a big NO-NO for you. Never proceed. Stop right there. You've got a lot of things you should learn about before stepping forward.

Do market research. It can help you in determining and proving your idea's potentials. You can gather relevant information from industry professionals, web researches, journals, government agencies' publications, social media platforms, and many more. A visit to the library with a few hours of surfing on the web could pave the way for you to understand your market deeply. Aim to gain a general sense of the type of customer your product or service will serve or at least be willing to find out through a thorough research process. You may follow Mevin's Walk, Talk, Note research process, as discussed above.

Make sure that your research plan should lay down the research objectives and give you the information you need to either proceed with your idea, fine-tune it, or take it back to the drawing board in the meantime.

Above all, never forget to prepare a list of questions you need to answer in your research and create a plan to answer them. Most importantly, to step up the business, I recommend that you set an appointment with your business consultant or an expert in the same industry, such as Melvin's advice. These experts can intelligently guide you on which type of research is the most appropriate. And, can further help you develop statistically valid samples, write questionnaires, and provide you with an objective and neutral source of information you need to gather depending on the type of product or service you want to sell and your overall research goals.

You can use such research to determine your potential market accurately, size up the competition, or test your product or service's usefulness and positioning. For example, if the product is a physical item, it is valuable to place it in the target market as a courtesy or donate it with an existing product on the market. For example, if selling a service can turn potential market awareness into a marketplace with crisp details through a website such as Google Ads, Social Media, and Emails, this can help create clear communication.

- **Analysis**

When working with firms on brand development, these brand developers first look at the business idea from four perspectives: company, customer, competitor, and collaborator. Let's discuss them in detail:

"THE RESILIENT ENTERPRISES"
Most Challenging 2021

Company: Think of your idea regarding your company's product/service's features—what benefits will it offer to your customers. What is your company's personality, and what key messages will you be relaying, including your promises to your customers.

Customer: There are three different customers you need to consider concerning your idea—first, the purchasers or those who decide or those who write the check. Second, the so-called influencers or those influence the people's purchasing decision—lastly, the end-users, or those that will be interested in your product.

Competitor: There are three different groups you have to keep in mind here: the primary, secondary, and tertiary. Placement in each level is base on (How business can compete with them) (How would tailor messaging when competing with each of these groups).

Collaborator: Think of some group of people you can collaborate with to boost your business. These people may be organizations, people who may have interest in your success but aren't pay or for any success, your business might have gained, such as associations, the media, and all other organizations capable of selling you to your customers.

- **SWOT Analysis**

Another approach you may consider in doing your research is the SWOT analysis, which means your business's intensive investigation of the following areas: S – your chosen industry's strengths, your product, or services. **W** – Your product's weakness, such as the design flaws or its price, is it competitive or reasonable? You need to check on those weaknesses and prepare plans to address them.

O – This refers to opportunities. What do you think are the opportunities that might happen? – This might come from outside your company, so it requires the right eye to see. It might be some developments in the market you are serving or improving the technology you are using. Whatever it is, spot them! These might give you a massive breakthrough in your business. Lastly, **T** – or the potential threats you might come across.

Proper SWOT analysis will enable you to comprehensively understand your business's strengths and flaws from internal information such as administration and organization, product development, and cost, including external factors such as foreign exchange rates, politics, and culture. It will assist you in realizing what fortune your business will make in the current market situation.

In whatever research approach you use to evaluate your idea, just be very sure to meet the research objectives you outlined for your product and service. Make it your top-of-mind. Do it the right way, and it will surely help you discover whether your idea has some holes that require patching.

- **Checking out the Competition**

Assuming that your research has successfully helped you unveil your competition, the next thing you need to do is to know more about them. Find out what's up to, I advise you to do it yourself, that's the best way you can do it. It means to be their

"THE RESILIENT ENTERPRISES"

Most Challenging 2021

mystery shopper. Observe the talk. Evaluate how they treat you, explore the whole place; its appearance, arrangements, system, and trend. Visit their website as well. Conduct formal research by yourself. Check on their social media accounts, if any. Check their Instagram; how many followers do they have? How often do they publish a post? And what content do they include in their ads? Spot some flaws if you can. Evaluate their service. Which area of it you think is poor? You can use that as a guide on how you will make your service an outstanding one. Find your selling point. Use all the data you've gathered.

For that step, it's also what's going to be what sets you apart and how to bait your customers straight to you.

You may be discouraged to find out that you're not quite ready to get started after spending time and money on the research already. Losing yourself won't help anyway, yet refocus your energy and learn more about why your idea needs more compressing. – that would be the best thing that you could do to predict the future and your success. For sure, you wouldn't want to hear that your baby is flawed, right? But, mind you, it is only through that feedback that you will know what needs improvements. Some companies even consider feedback as a gift. It's a stepping stone towards success in disguise.

You may fail. Don't panic yet. Just keep in mind that some ideas simply need some modifications. Before you start flipping through your idea books again, consider whether or not you can make this idea work. For sure, there was a reason why you thought of that idea in the first place. Think back, then reconsider things. Well, some ideas might seem they'll end up a total dud, only to find out that after doing a little research, such an idea end up being a great success. This is precisely the reason why ideas that seem like a flop will always be interesting to me.

I've seen many people who launch ideas that I thought were beyond foolish, but later on, I learned more about the concept, the customer, and the vision. Then I realized the real risk is taking.

Sometimes when we look into an idea, we may find that success was just luck. But the real score is that when we try to revisit it several times, you will realize that the founder had some clear insights about its potential, where he focused, which eventually led him to success.

- **When is your idea, ready to go?**

Thus far, the market research you have conducted has to be a good indicator of where to go next with your idea. One huge factor to consider, though, is your price. You might want to do it competitively while thinking, at the same time, what the market will bear. So, for products or services that have a close competitor, here's what I can say, your pricing should always be dependent on your market research, especially on the competition of the same product or service in the market. Reconsider the uniqueness and credibility of your work. It can put you in a higher position on the same market even at a high price.

As a professional business adviser and strategist, you must take business consultation: I would honestly recommend talking with an experienced business consultant for expert advice in any relevant industry. Being professionals in this field, these consultants have performed well in the market while doing their expertise with proven track records. And because investing in a business is a huge decision to make

"THE RESILIENT ENTERPRISES"
Most Challenging 2021

with your preferred business consultant, you can talk about each detail of your business when consulting the model's concept. This branding is an extensive work. But you can go along smoothly with a professional business consultant with you.

So, what does 'consulting' mean in business?

The definition is straightforward. Consulting is defining as the act of giving advice done by expert people with some experiences in specific fields, commonly about financial or business matters. That's it. A consultant provides expert advice professionally, of course, with some level of expertise in specific fields. A group of people finds it valuable and willing to pay the fee to access their knowledge. Business consultants never use the word "problem." It doesn't exist in their vocabulary. Instead, they talk about it as opportunities to enhance value. Try to ask a consultant what they do. y\You will likely get the answer by saying, "I'm in the solutions business," despite the criticisms lingering around every consultant. Their expertise can genuinely add value to your middle-market company. Still, you also need to know when and why you should use them. There is a massive range of business issues that consultants can provide solutions to Different types of consultants bring other ideas to the table, laid with various points of view.

Engaging a consultant's services can improve your business' performance and make relevant changes to achieve success.

Consultants are there to help companies overcome challenges, increase potential revenue, or grow as a whole. Make sure to hire a consultant with prior relevant experience, though. And, if possible, one who has initial success with companies like yours.

Furthermore, business consultants provide management consulting also to help organizations improve their performance and efficiency. They analyse businesses and create solutions while assisting companies in meeting their goals at the same time. Thus, business owners should consider hiring business consultants if they need help or looking at their potentials from another perspective or a catalyst for some relevant changes in their companies.

- **Reasons for hiring a Consultant**

Now that you know the types of consultants, let us know why you need one. Here are five common reasons:

Rent a brain: hire a consultant if you don't have the human resources you need for some reason; perhaps one is because some internal personnel has quit. You don't need to have the consultant on full-time. You may hire one temporarily instead of filling in the gap until a full-time internal person is hiring. Hiring a consultant can make the breaking of the relationship easy and cost-effective.

Manage Change: consultants, aside from giving expert advice, are also adept at withstanding disapproval and fostering Change in an organization. So, if your mid-sized company has prevalent internal squabbling concerning imminent changes, then bringing in a consultant can break the deadlock. Consultants are aware that they're seldom being brought in for political cover and will shoulder the blame for unpopular changes such as reducing headcounts and other cost-cutting measures.

"THE RESILIENT ENTERPRISES"
Most Challenging 2021

Teach and implement best practices: so, it isn't straightforward to invent techniques, especially when you start. The question is, why develop one? When lots of consultants have already implemented some with various clients. Consultants aren't only expert academically and theoretically. They have so much exposure to the actual applications, too, as they also work directly with leading companies to implement Change.

Infuse Creativity: consultants may have fresh perspectives on your business. Thus, having an outsider come in to give you additional inputs, such as more ideas, is of great help. Sometimes, in-house people are too narrow-minded and too close to the company that they fail to consider a different standpoint to examine the bigger picture within your market. Hence, consultants are there to give you valuable insights capable of boosting your internal creative thinking.

Deliver Training: consultants are born trainers. So, you can tell them to share knowledge with you about almost everything. They're a perfect choice to do a training course with or a day-long presentation for your company in virtually any area. They blend theory and practice, and that's what a good consultant is. And, this attribute of a good consultant can deliver high value to your midmarket company.

While it is true that engaging the services of a consultant can be expensive, you just need to weigh the cost versus benefits.

What will you get back if you hire one? – will it pay off to hire their services? Absolutely yes in all aspects. You can never go wrong, getting your company a good consultant.

"THE RESILIENT ENTERPRISES"

Most Challenging 2021

- **Types of Consultants**

Business consultants generally add value to your middle-market business, particularly in five major areas as follows:

Management and strategy: excellent consultants have a deep understanding of different markets, so they should bring the best practices from other industries to your company. If you wish to expand your needs geographically, consider extending your portfolio by reorganizing your middle-market company to promote efficiency and cost-effectiveness. If you can, buy out a smaller competitor. It might also increase your overall capabilities, including hiring an experienced management/strategy consultant; it would make great sense.

Operations: now, if you wish to improve the quality and efficiency of your production processes, some consultants are specializing in it, a service called business process re-engineering – this means they come in, then map out your existing processes, analyse opportunities for reducing the number of steps in that process while still maintaining quality, and re-engineer your processes in such a way that diminishes efforts and costs. On the other hand, other consultants specialize in quality control systems, potentially helping you make changes in reducing defects.

IT: this is a fast-growing consulting area since the demand for new technology impacts middle-market companies every day.

To develop a new system or integrate an old system and work together, an IT consultant can help. IT consultants can help you make your IT more flexible to meet internal and external customers' dynamic demands effectively.

"THE RESILIENT ENTERPRISES"
Most Challenging 2021

HR: how about improving the overall satisfaction of your employees? Recruit top talent, and retain top performers. In this area, you should come to an HR consultant. – They specialize in developing compensation strategies which relate to your business goals, Training, developing your people in areas such as business communication and leadership. Thus, they can surely help you improve performance-related feedback and evaluation to your team to make your employees work smarter.

Marketing: for your marketing-related concerns, a marketing consultant is of help. Be it for your company's new logo needs, perhaps a unique market position for one of your brands, a new social media strategy to interact with your customers. This is where marketing consultants specialize. They can indeed offer you a creative spark when your people have run out of one. They will let you see what other companies have done to attract more customers.

How can I find a Business Consultant?

Looking for the right business consultant is perhaps the most challenging task for the business owner or the management, for we all want to hire an ideal consultant. And a perfect business consultant is passionate and works with dedication, one who drives excellence. More importantly, make sure to pick one who has expertise in your business' industry, who experienced the kinds of problems your business faces or might face. If you could ensure they have strong referrals that would be even great.

Furthermore, make sure to check the necessary certificates relevant to your industry. Examine your prospected business consultant through their website or any materials they have.

"THE RESILIENT ENTERPRISES"

Most Challenging 2021

Look for images and well-documented information about their services. It could help a lot to request past documented successes and speak to those businesses concerned to verify.

What is the typical background to look for in a business consultant?

The right background you should look for in a consultant you need depends on your chosen business industry. That consultant can be someone who is into management, one who is scientifically-equipped, or one who is technically knowledgeable. Say, if you need someone who could help your company develop new proprietary software or computer-based workflow, then you might want to engage in a technical business consultant. Companies usually hire a management consultant's services for outside specific needs as they want to improve customer satisfaction or employee morale and their bottom line.

But, regardless of the type of consultant you engage, their backgrounds are critical. It will help improve your business in almost all areas. So, here are the things you need to consider when reviewing potential consultants:

- **Do they have hands-on experience?**

This is not only critical, but a MUST to know. If you could look for someone who has successfully owned or run a small business, or at least an enterprise organization, or perhaps just specific departments, then could be a great fit.

- **Are their experiences relevant?**

As discussed above, the background you should look for in a consultant you need is entirely dependent upon your business'

"THE RESILIENT ENTERPRISES"
Most Challenging 2021

industry. Thus, his experiences' relevance to your business is a MUST. While a former bank CEO may seem inviting and impressive, a question follows: would his affairs in such a field make sense in yours? – Point is, does he have that capability and required knowledge to turn your cupcake into a profitable small business? Perhaps they could. But in this case, if you could come across a consultant who is only a former restaurant owner but is now successfully helping small eatery owners make a living, then this one might best fit your business' needs and goals. Just make sure to pick one who has worked in the same industry as yours and, if possible, one who has a business that matches yours in terms of size, style, needs, and goals.

- **What's their track record with consulting?**

Don't just look after the experiences, though, as discussed. You should also need to consider prior successes they have demonstrated in the same businesses as yours. Never miss asking for their portfolios, especially the portfolio of the list of brands the consultant has worked for—request their references. Make sure to look for a consultant who has helped businesses overcome various challenges your business might encounter. Above all, look for those who have grown businesses similar to yours. Reach for their former clients with whom they had successful engagements with Talk to them to know more about how satisfied they were with the consultant's services.

What do consultants do?

There are different reasons why business owners should hire business consultants. It's because they offer a wide range of services which includes, but not limited to, the following:

"THE RESILIENT ENTERPRISES"
Most Challenging 2021

- Providing expertise in a specific market;
- Identifying problems;
- Supplementing existing staff;
- Change initiator;
- Provides objectivity;
- Acts as teachers and trainers for employees;
- Does the "dirty work" like terminating staff;
- They save organizations by reviving it;
- Innovators who create new business;
- Influencers influence people.

First of all, the business consultant discovers everything at the onset; thus, the first stage in their career as a consultant of any company is the discovery phase. Here, a business consultant unveils all its relevant information from its mission and vision down to its goals. They take time to learn about the business as much as possible because a consultant shouldn't miss any information about the company he is serving. So, he needs to know everything about it, from the business owner down to its employees, especially its board of directors, then has a facility tour to learn every detail. Then, most importantly, they analyse the company's finances and read all materials the company has. This is a crucial stage; it's as essential as doing market analysis when starting a business. A consultant is not expecting to serve better a company he barely knows. Thus, when you engage a consultant's services, make sure that he is making efforts to know your business at the very onset.

After completing the discovery stage, the business consultant jumps into the next step, called the evaluation phase. Here, the consultant identifies where Change is needed, including all the SWOT, its strengths, weaknesses, and further opportunities and the foreseeable problems that may include the ownership issues and management concerns that might be identifying already. And also, such new problems the consultant discovers as a result of objectivity. Furthermore, in identifying opportunities, the consultant should locate the possibilities of growing the business more, including ways to increase profits and boost efficiency.

More than just identifying potential problems, the consultant should also develop solutions to those foreseen problems and create plans to capitalize on opportunities and make the company benefit from it. If the company has a strong sales department but is weak in marketing, this is an excellent chance for the company to increase marketing resources and capitalize on the sales staff. Open and transparent communication between the consultant and the company's employees is essential during this phase.

Productive Criticism

At this stage, the business should not take the consultant's criticism personally, as it is instead a constructive one being a fresh viewpoint from him. It could cause an obstacle to positive changes, which isn't going to be helpful. Instead, the business owner should have feedback, provide opinions to the business consultant, and consider revising plans as necessary.

After the consultant and the business owner agree, the consultant is then ready to proceed to the next stage of consulting called the 'restructuring phase or the plan's implementation stage. In this phase, the consultant builds assets and abolishes liabilities. They are on close monitoring of the plan's progress and adjusts it accordingly as the need arises.

"THE RESILIENT ENTERPRISES"

Most Challenging 2021

Build a Business Plan: after consulting with a professional business consultant, make sure to get all the relevant details of your business, then comprehensively plan your business with your consultant.

Before a business can borrow money in a bank, a business plan needs to be presenting. Hence, to say a company needs an initial business plan is an understatement. It is a MUST. You should never miss preparing one, or you will stumble along the way with no reason to get up.

Sound business plans usually show highly detailed information about the business, including, among others, its industry, marketing aspect, finance, personnel, and various operating procedures.

- **Main Components of a Business Plan**

Do not complicate your business plans. Make it as simple as possible. Keep it short but complete and understandable if you can. Below is a step by step procedure you may use as a guide in smoothly creating your needed business plans with less complexity.

A Business Plan has six components: raising money or just trying to figure out if your idea is viable.

A reliable Business Plan covers all these six essential topics, which we will discuss in detail as you go along. For now, here's a quick overview of what to expect about each case. But, before we jump into that, let us talk first about the three rules that make business planning easier.

Before you kick start creating your business plan, here are the three rules you need to learn first. Always make it a goal to get

"THE RESILIENT ENTERPRISES"
Most Challenging 2021

your business plan finished so you can focus on building your business. Check the directions below:

- **Keep it short:**

Do note; no one is going to read a business plan that looks like a novel. Thus, every business plan should be just simple. Short but concise. Remember that it functions as your tool to run and grow your business. Hence, briefly prepared Business Plans are not only ideal but also suitable for glances at every once in a while, as the need arises in building your business. Consider it as something you will continue using as you go along. Thus, it requires consistent revisions and improvements as you see fit. Hence, an excessively long business plan is a huge hassle to review and revise. Each time, you would want to glance at it, and it will surely take you forever before you could find what you need to read. Most likely, will keet it in a drawer until it can never see it.

- **Know your audience:**

Consider that you need to have your business plan understood by your reader. Thus, make sure to know who your audiences are and use the appropriate language they will surely understand.

For example, if your company is trying to develop a complex coding solution process, and your prospective investors aren't software engineers or technologists, then using highly technical terms will be burdensome for them to understand. These are, for sure unfamiliar to them. Avoid using them then.

Keep your wordings direct and straightforward. Make sure your investors will find them accommodating. To be safe, use terms that everyone can understand.

"THE RESILIENT ENTERPRISES"

Most Challenging 2021

- **Don't be intimidated:**

Keep in mind that the majority of business owners aren't experts in their chosen fields. Only a few of them hold MBA degrees, some might have accounting degrees, but you can count them. There's no reason to be intimidated. Like how you will surely do it, they just learn everything little by little as they go along using some useful tools to help them.

Writing a business plan may seem too challenging to do as how it sounds. But it doesn't have to be. Don't make it too hard for yourself. 'You know your business more than anyone else does. You are the expert on it in the first place. That thought alone gives you a reason to take a deep breath and take it all easy. It's not going to be as challenging as you think.

And, to make you feel all at ease, you don't have to start with a full, detailed business plan. It can be easier to start with a simple business plan. One that you can shortly describe the process very plainly, which the reader can easily understand. It is called a lean project. After this, go back and start building a longer, more detailed one.

Let me explain in detail every segmentation of your worth-reading business plan. We'll discuss here what should be included in your business plan, as well as what to skip, including the most critical financial projections.

1. Executive Summary:

This section of your business plan introduces your company. Explain your engagements what you're looking for from your readers. Technically this serves as your chapter one. While it is absolutely the first thing that your target readers will read, write it out, I would insist. I would advise you to do that. That's the ideal. Keep going and find out why.

Knowing every detail of your business inside out prepares you to write your business plan's executive summary better. This section covers the summary of everything else in your business plan.

Ideally, the executive summary, for some purposes, can act as a standalone document that contains the highlights of your detailed plan. Some investors who want to evaluate your business would only ask you to give them the executive summary of your business plan. And, that commonly happens. If they saw what they would like to see, then usually a request asking for the entire business plan follows, including a pitch presentation and more detailed financial documents for them to examine thoroughly.

And, since it's a crucial component of your business plan. A clear, brief, but concise executive summary is ideal. Make sure only to cover the key highlights of your business. Don't aim for a too detailed one. A perfect executive summary is mostly a two-paged document only at most, designed as such for quick reads that draw interest and makes your investors feel eager to know more.

What consists of a winning Executive Summary?

So, a winning executive summary is one that contains the following components:

- **One sentence business overview**

This is the first sentence you need to write right under your business name at the top of the right page, which should be a sentence that sums up the essence of what you are doing. – it can be a tagline. But it could be more effective if the sentence exactly describes what your company does, known as your value proposition.

- **Problem**

Make a summary of your problem in the market in at least one or two sentences. Because technically, every business aims to solve a problem for its customers and fill a need in the market that you should specify in your executive summary.

- **Solution**

Solution refers to a product or service, which will be your solution in addressing the problem in the market you have identified.

- **Target Market**

Come to think of your ideal customers or the group of people you intend to serve; they are your target market. – make sure to be specific in indicating them. Say, you're putting up a shoe company. You can't state everyone to be your target just because everyone has feet. No! – make it as specific as having a segment as much as possible, such as 'runners' for one. It will make your strategies easy to generate, such as marketing and sales efforts. And you likely attract easily the types of customers who will most likely buy your products.

- **Competition**

Competition doesn't excuse any business in the market. And, it is crucial to provide an overview of yours in your executive summary. Briefly explain how your target market is solving its problems today. State whether alternatives or substitutes exist from which they can choose.

- **Company Overview and Team**

Technically, your most competitive idea still has space in the trash without the right people to execute them properly, which is why an investor takes the team into massive consideration. They stand on "an idea will remain an idea without the right team to make it a reality.

Thus, never miss the part where you introduce a brief overview of your team and a quick catch why you and your team are the right people to present your idea to the market.

2. Financial Summary:

Clearly state here your financial plans, specifically highlighting critical aspects of it.

It must always come with a chart showing your projected sales, expenses, as well as profitability.

- **Funding Requirement**

This section is intended for business owners to create a business plan to secure bank loans or those waiting for an angel in disguise in the person of investors or capitalists. – make sure to include what you need in the executive summary without further providing potential investment related to future negotiations. Just a brief statement of how much exactly do you need to raise.

"THE RESILIENT ENTERPRISES"
Most Challenging 2021

- **Milestones and Traction**

Opportunity

The four main chapters of a business plan include opportunity, execution, company overview, and financial plan. In the opportunity chapter of your business plan is where the total score of your project resides. This chapter includes information about the problem you are soon solving and your solution to the identified problem. The group of people you plan to sell your products to Lastly, how your product and service will survive the existing competitive landscape shall also be included herein.

Consider including in the section also your edge among others that sets your solution apart. Briefly state how you plan to expand your offerings in the future.

Although from your executive summary, your readers are expecting to have a picture of your business. As it's where you expand your initial overview stated in the executive summary, specifically providing details and answering questions that you won't be able to cover in the executive summary.

- **The Problem and Solution**

Begin this chapter by clearly describing what problems you are solving for your customers. Indicate what their primary pain point is and what they do to solve them. – Perhaps this solution they have in their hands is too expensive; check them out.

Clearly stating the problem, you are solving for your customers is a stepping stone for your business's success. And, it is by far the most critical element of a business plan.

"THE RESILIENT ENTERPRISES"
Most Challenging 2021

Be very careful about the information you have, though. Ensure that the problems you want to solve for your potential customers are real ones, not merely theoretical issues. In business planning, one effective way you can do to make sure that you come up with valid information is to do it yourself literally. Take time to step away from your computer for a while and reach out to your potential customers. Validate the assumed problems at hand then, figure out whether your formulated possible solutions fit them.

After clearly stating your target market's problem, discuss in the following section your solution. – This section specifically refers to your product or service as your offered solution. Briefly talk about what it is basically and how do you plan to provide. Discuss further how exactly it will solve problems.

Other business owners might want to consider using a real user's honest feedback by telling a story about it. In such a case, you should be willing to pay.

Once you are sure who your customers are, make a rough draft of how many are there in the market and find out if they are enough for your business. If not, you just bumped into a warning sign.

- **Target Market**

Now that you have entirely discussed your identified problem and potential solutions think of your target market again and specify to whom you are selling

This section does not need much detailed information.

"THE RESILIENT ENTERPRISES"
Most Challenging 2021

- **Market Analysis and Market Research**

A market analysis starts with market research. – Market segments have to be identified first. Next, determine the size of each component. Determine the size of each market.

A market segment is a group of people (or other businesses) who you have the potential to sell products or services to.

Don't be among those business owners who fell on the trap of labelling their market as "everyone," though. While it is easy to say that you target "everyone" as your market, a shoe company stating 'everyone with a foot' is their demand will not be practicable. One edge, every successful business person does is to target a specific segment of the market. Say, given an example: the shoe company, a particular component such as athletes, would be ideal.

- **TAM, SAM, and SOM**

This refers to the classic method of identifying a target market that will allow you to look at the market sizes from a top-down approach and a bottom-up approach. – with this approach, you will formulate a good business plan with a well-identified target market, which provides some data that indicates how fast each segment is growing.

Check their definitions below:

TAM stands for **T**otal **A**vailable or addressable **M**arket – this refers to everyone you wish to reach with your product.

SAM stands for **S**egmented **A**ddressable **M**arket or simply your 'served available market.' And this covers the portion of TAM you will target; and,

"THE RESILIENT ENTERPRISES"
Most Challenging 2021

SOM stands for **S**hare **o**f the **M**arket, and this refers to the subset of your SAM that you will realistically reach, most likely in the first few years of your business.

After identifying your key markets, discuss their trends, such as whether or not they are growing. Above all, discuss their evolving needs, tastes, and other potential changes in the market.

Who are your Ideal Customers?

You identify who your ideal customers for each segment are coming after you have placed your target market segments.

And the most appropriate way to discuss your ideal customers in your business plan is to use your "buyer persona" or the "user persona." These terms are the fictitious representation of your market. They have their names, gender, income level, likes, dislikes, and so on.

While this means an additional task for you to do, you should never underestimate how useful this tool will be for you, especially in identifying your marketing and sales tactics you will need to attract your ideal customers.

- **Key Customers**

You should discuss this in the final section of your target market section. It is not that important and only required for huge companies with very few customers. If you are starting up a typical small business, you may skip this.

But if you are into B2B marketing, you may have few customers crucial for your business's success, or perhaps a handful of customers who are trend leaders in your space. Use this final portion of your target market chapter to discuss those specific customers and provide details about how important they are to your business' success.

- **Competition**

Immediately after discussing your target market is where you should concern about your competition. Talk about who else can solve your target customer's pain points. The spotlight when talking about what your competitive advantages are among these competitors, and illustrate as much as possible how your solution is different amongst them and why yours is a better option your potential customers should choose. A 'competitor Matrix' is used by most business owners to compare business plans to their competitors. – a potential investor might want to know what advantages you have over the competition and how you plan on differentiating yourself.

One biggest mistake an entrepreneur could make in his business plan is stating his business doesn't belong to any competition.

When in reality, all businesses have competition. It may not be one who appears to be a direct competition that exists when a competitor offers a similar solution like yours. Take note that there is an 'indirect competition,' which happens when the customers solve their problems in a different kind of solution.

Let us take Henry Ford as an example. When he was first marketing his cars, he got significantly few direct competitions as there weren't any other car manufacturers yet. But there were different modes of transportation like horses, bikes, trains, and people seldom walking as means. At first glance, none of these appears in direct competition, but they are considered people's alternatives to solve their transportation problems.

- **Future products and services**

Every entrepreneur holds a vision in them of where their business is heading in the long run. While we all want to spend a lot of time exploring future opportunities for new product innovations, it's not going to be ideal to discuss these ideas more in your business plan. What's useful is only one or two paragraphs about your potential projects, just to show investors where you foresee your business in the long-range plans. Don't be overpowered by long-term goals that already sounds difficult for you to complete. Your entire focus should be on successfully bringing your first product or service into the market.

- **Execution**

Now that you have laid down your opportunity chapter. Execution chapter begins – in this chapter, you will discuss your marketing and sales plans, including your operations and how you'll measure success. The key milestones you expect to achieve are also being discussed here.

- **Marketing and Sales Plan**

This part of your business plan is where you should show in detail how you plan to reach your target market segments, also called target marketing. State and discuss how you plan to sell to those, introduce your pricing plan, and what types of activities and partnerships you need to make your business a success.

"THE RESILIENT ENTERPRISES"
Most Challenging 2021

It is imperative that you already have your target market well defined and have your buyer persona(s) laid down even before you think of writing your marketing plan. Because if you don't understand who you are marketing to, then your business plan will have less value and might end up a piece of scratch.

- **Your positioning Statement**

This will be the first part of your marketing and sales plan wherein you will be discussing how you will present your company to your customers. Let them know whether you could be their low-price solution, or will your resolution be among the premium or luxury brands in your market. Highlight for them what your competitors don't have that you possess.

Before you proceed to work on your positioning statement, take a moment to evaluate the current market by answering the following question:

- What features do you offer that your competitors don't have?
- What are your customer's primary needs and wants?
- How are your competitors positioning themselves?
- How do you plan on differentiating yourself from the competition?
- To make it simple, just simply answer the question: why should your customer choose you among others?
- Lastly, the most crucial question is, where do you see your company in the landscape of other solutions?

After you come up with your answers, you can then work on your positioning strategies and clearly define them in your business plan.

"THE RESILIENT ENTERPRISES"
Most Challenging 2021

Your positioning statement doesn't have to be long or in-depth. Just briefly explain where your company sits within the competitive landscape. Discuss your core value position, highlighting what differentiates it from the alternatives that your customer might consider.

You might want to consider this simple formula below to develop your positioning statement:

For [*target market description*]

Who [target *market need*], [*this product*] [*how it meets the need*]

Unlike [*key competition*],

it [*most important distinguishing feature*]

- **Pricing**

Pricing comes next after completing your overall positioning strategy.

Your positioning strategy is what drives how you price your offerings.

Price directs a powerful message to the consumers and can be an essential tool to communicate your positioning to the consumers. Say, if you are offering a premium product, a premium price transmits the message to your consumers.

Like an art with some rules to follow, deciding on your price goes the same. The rules to consider are as follows:

- **Covering your costs**

In most cases, you should be charging your customers more than it costs you to deliver your product or service, subject to certain exceptions, though.

"THE RESILIENT ENTERPRISES"
Most Challenging 2021

- **Primary and secondary profit centre pricing**

Your introductory price may not be your primary profit centre. An example would be selling a product at or even below your cost. It requires much more profitable maintenance to go along.

- **Matching the market rate**

Your prices should match the demand and expectations of your consumer. Having a relatively high price may result in having no customers. Likewise, too low prices may undervalue your offerings. Strategize your pricing approach in different ways. To help you develop the right strategy, you may consider the following:

- **Cost-plus Pricing**

Pricing this way is done by getting your total cost first, then mark up. This applies effectively to manufacturers as covering initial expenses is crucial.

- **Market-based pricing**

This pricing method considers the current landscape of competitors then price based on what the market is expecting. You may price at the high-end or low-end of the need to establish your positioning.

- **Value Pricing**

This pricing method is another way of determining your price by considering how much value you provide to your customer.

"THE RESILIENT ENTERPRISES"

Most Challenging 2021

- **Promotion**

Having laid down your pricing and positioning in the previous section, the promotion strategy has to be discussing this time.

A promotion plan explains how you plan on communicating with your prospects and customers. Ensure that promotional programs that aren't profitable are hard to maintain in the long run. Thus, you need to measure how much your promotions cost and how much sales they generate.

- **Packaging**

The packaging is just as important as how you need to wear appropriate clothes. – The same goes for selling a product. The packaging of that product is crucial. Hence, if you have images of your packaging, it's a great deal to consider its inclusion in your business plan. Along with the pictures, ensure that the packaging section in your business plan answers the following questions:

Does it match your positioning strategy?

In what way does it communicate your fundamental proposition?

Is the packaging a competitive one?

- **Advertising**

An overview of the types of advertising you plan to spend your money on should be included in your business plan. Will online advertising be part of your considerations? How about offline media?

"THE RESILIENT ENTERPRISES"
Most Challenging 2021

Among the contents your business plan has, one key component worth-highlighting is your plan for measuring the success of your advertising.

- **Public Relations**

One great way to reach customers is by getting digital media to cover you. Besides, getting a prominent review of your product or service can give you the exposure you need to grow your business.

Thus, if you intend public relations as part of your promotional strategy, consider discussing it here.

- **Content Marketing**

This strategy is becoming more and more popular promotion strategy nowadays.

A reliable plan is what describes content marketing. – it's when you publish useful information, tips, and advice, usually made available for free for purposes of engaging your target market to get to know your company more through the expertise you delivered.

It is all about teaching and educating your prospects on topics that they might be interested in, more than the features and benefits you offer.

Social Media

As a result of the enormous growth in digital marketing, social media presence gradually became an essential requirement. No business should miss having one, or the previous era will drag you back.

"THE RESILIENT ENTERPRISES"
Most Challenging 2021

It does not necessarily mean that you have to be on every social networking site we have, though. Being on the ones your target customers are on is the most important. You can't miss a single customer checking you on to measure how responsive you are.

- **Strategic Associations**

You might want to consider partnerships as part of your marketing plan as well. This is what strategic associations are all about, This may help you, one way or another, to give access to a target market segment for your company and allowing your partner to offer a new product or service to their customers simultaneously.

If you have existing partnerships already established, it will also make sense to discuss it in detail in your business plan.

- **Operations**

Your business works are all discussed in this section with complete details: Basically, the discussion contains the logistics, technology, and other nuts and bolts. Depending on what type of business you are starting, you may or may not need the succeeding sections. Include what you want, leave all the rest.

- **Sourcing and fulfilment**

If the products you are selling are from another vendor, make sure to include your products and how they deliver them to you. Above all, state how the products will be providing to your customers. That's basically what sourcing and fulfilment are.

Furthermore, if your products are sourced from manufacturers overseas, make it clear for the investors to know your progress working with these suppliers. And if your company will deliver your products to your customers, describe your plans for shipping your products.

- **Technology**

If you are in a technology company, make sure to include in your business plan what your "secret sauce is" – it doesn't mean you have to divulge trade secrets in your business plan. Instead, state clearly how your technology is advantageous to all others out there, especially those lodged in the market. At most, consider discussing how your technology works. – you don't have to include every detail about it, though. For if an investor is interested to know more, they will surely ask for it. You may include such information in your appendix.

Remember that your goal is to make your business plan as simple as possible. It could easily make your plan too long to explain too much detail here. We need to avoid that.

- **Distribution**

This section is a must for product companies' business plans. Thus, service companies may skip this.

Distribution is how you hand in your products to your customer. Thus, distribution channels vary among businesses. Formulating your distribution plan is done best by interviewing others of the same industry as yours, so you could figure out what distribution models they have.

To give you hints on what distribution channels are, you might want to consider the following models:

Direct distribution

Selling directly to consumers is the example that best describes it. – it also by far the most straightforward and most profitable mode of distribution.

The direct distribution channel is organized and managed by the manufacturer. Direct channels are more expensive to build early and can sometimes require significant capital investment. Warehousing, logistics systems, trucks, and delivery personnel will need to be preparing. However, once these channels are established, direct channels may be smaller and less expensive than the indirect channel.

Direct selling can be difficult to test on a large scale, but it often allows the manufacturer to connect with the website founder.

By controlling all parts of the distribution channel, the manufacturer has more control over exporting goods. They have more power than reducing vulnerability, adding new functionality, and setting values

- Direct distribution is a direct path to the customer where the developer manages all aspects of the distribution
- The direct distribution provides other companies with control over the entire system.

Retail distribution

Dealing with thousands of individual suppliers is not only burdensome to large retailers but also one huge hassle. – thus, they would instead opt to buy through large distribution companies that aggregate products—from various suppliers, making the inventory available for retailers to purchase. Of course, these distributors take a percentage of the sales that pass through their warehouses.

- **Manufacturers' Representatives**

These are typically salespeople who work for a 'repping' agency. They usually work on a commission basis. They sell your products into an appropriate channel as they often have relationships with both distributors and retailers.

- **OEM**

This stands for "original equipment manufacturer." Thus, if your product sold to another company that incorporates your work into their finished product, you will use an OEM channel.

One good example to cite is a large auto manufacturer who, while building large components of their cars, also consider purchasing common parts from third-party vendors and incorporating them into their finished vehicle.

While there are various channels you may choose from, take note though you are not limited to picking a single track. Some companies use combinations of them as part of their plans. For example, selling directly through distributors is a prevalent combined channel. Apple, for one. You can purchase one from the apple store now or at a target store.

Milestones and Metrics

A Business Plan is just a piece of paper without any real path to get the works done, complete with a schedule, define roles, and critical responsibilities.

"THE RESILIENT ENTERPRISES"
Most Challenging 2021

This section does not need to belong. However, you must look forward and schedule the next vital steps for your business. Investors will indeed evaluate how deep is your understanding of what needs to happen to make your plans a reality and that the schedules you set are realistic ones.

Milestones are planned significant goals. For example, if you are engaged in producing consumer products, your milestones can be finding manufacturers and first-order receipt. Another example has medical devices; milestones could be clinical testing and government approval processes.

- **Traction**

While we look forward to milestones, we also need to consider tracing backwards, and that's what traction is all about. – it means, as you move forward, keep looking back as well, like trace before all your significant accomplishments. Investors will surely like to read about them as they serve as your first success shreds of evidence.

It could come in the form of initial sales, perhaps pilot programs, or some significant partnerships. Sharing them could be your catch as it could show to what extent your success could be. Thus, they hold part of your business plan's critical points too.

- **Metrics**

This refers to the numbers you will keep your eyes on regularly to keep track of your business' health. They serve as the drivers of growth for your business model and your business plan. It will allow you to have a real-time observation of real change and enable you to discern potential trouble early.

Thus, you must include every detail of your business metrics in your business plan.

- **Key Assumptions and Risks**

Lastly, your business plan should have the key assumptions you have made that are important for your business' success.

One way of formulating assumptions is to take into consideration risks. Think of the risks you are taking with your business. Say, if you don't have a proven demand for a new product, perhaps you assume that people will want what you are building. Another thing is when you are relying on online advertising as your primary promotional channel. You are considering the costs of that advertising and the percentage of ad viewers who will purchase.

In most cases, your business assumptions are what take failure and success apart. When you recognize your beliefs, you can set out things to prove that your opinions are all right. And this guide you to minimize assumptions as well, which leads your business to success all the more.

Company Overview and Team

In this chapter, you will introduce the structure of your company and who the team members are. These details are crucial for investors to know as they would want to know whose behind who will translate such a good idea into a reigning business.

- **Team**

As the old maxim goes, "investors don't invest in ideas, they invest in people." This never goes out of tune. Some would

"THE RESILIENT ENTERPRISES"

Most Challenging 2021

even exaggerate the idea by saying they would instead invest in a mediocre idea with great people behind a blockbuster idea with poor brains behind.

To make the idea simple, it means a successful business all comes down to who's behind, taking what's in the paper into action. It's merely a discussion of whether an idea should be accomplished and whether you have the right team in place to turn the drawing into action. Are the ones that could make your business a great one that will keep your customers banging on your doors? A question worth noting.

This is the chapter where you should give your best shot in stating that you have the right team to make your idea a reality. It should further show the essential roles and responsibilities your business needs to reach success.

Also, include brief bios that highlight the relevant experiences of each key team member. What's more important here is to showcase why your team is the right team to turn the idea into a reality. Include your statements if they have the right industry experiences and background and if they had entrepreneurial success before.

One common mistake a neophyte entrepreneur commits in describing the management team is giving everyone a C-level title such as CEO, CMO, COO, CFO, etc. While this might be good for images, frequently, it can't be realistic. − As the company grows, it might need various experiences and knowledge in specific fields to be required. Thus, it would be ideal to allow room for the growth of titles rather than start at the top without space for future development or change.

"THE RESILIENT ENTERPRISES"
Most Challenging 2021

Technically, you don't have to stress out having a complete management team to have a comprehensive business plan. Suppose you find any management team gaps; that's fine. Investors get that you know you are missing certain key people as a sign of maturity and knowledge about your business's success. If you do have gaps in your team at the onset, indicate it in the plan. – identify who these people are, clearly state that you are looking for the right people to fill such relevant roles.

Finally, having accomplished everything, as discussed above. Including a proposed organizational chart is your next key consideration in moving forward with your business plan. This isn't that critical as you think, though, as can just leave this in your business plan's appendix. But, as you go on fund hunting, you will indeed be asked for an organizational chart. Thus, it is still better to have one. Furthermore, beyond merely trying to raise money, your organizational chart is also a useful tool to help you think about your company and how to grow it over time.

- **Company Overview**

The shortest section of every business plan is. Thus, if your goal is intended only for business partners and team members, you may skip this part.

But, for a plan intended for external people, this section of your business plan should include specific details as follows:

1. Mission statement;
2. Intellectual property;
3. A review of your company's legal structure and ownership;
4. The business location;

5. A brief history of the company if it's an existing company.

Mission Statement

A company mission statement should be short, one or two sentences at most. Short as it should be, it should also be encompassing what you are trying to do at a very high level. Your overall value proposition and your mission statement might be the same thing.

A generic statement is one thing to be avoided when framing your mission statement. Avoiding talking about how you will serve your customers and your employees makes your mission statement too long.

- **Location**

Lastly, the company overview section should also describe your current location, including the areas of all the facilities that your company owns.

This is important for businesses that serve consumers from a storefront and industries that require extensive facilities, manufacturing, warehousing, and all others alike that have a location. This information holds an essential part of your business plan.

Financial Plan

Finally, a company's overview will never be complete without this section. Although this used to be the most challenging part of preparing, every entrepreneur finds it the same. But it doesn't have to be as intimidating as it sounds. In fact, for most start-ups, it's less complicated than you seem. Without a degree in business, you could build up a stable financial forecast. Although, should you need back up doing one, plenty of tools and resources are ubiquitous to help you build up your solid financial plan.

A typical financial plan displays monthly sales, revenue forecasts for the first 12 months, and the annual projections for the remaining three to five years. Typically, a three-year projection is satisfactory, but some investors would require a five-year forecast, challenging.

To guide you prepare yours, here are standard financial statement details your business plan should have. It's a guide for you with a brief overview of what each section should have.

- **Sales Forecast**

Your projection of how much you will sell over the next few years is basically what your sales forecast should discuss in it.

In forecasting sales, focus on the high-level for now. Do not make it too complicated for you with the possibility of ending up committing an error in detail. Consider that a sales forecast is typically broken down into several rows, with a row for each core product or service you offer.

Say, for a restaurant, could break down forecasting into groups such as lunch, dinner, and drinks. Whereas, if you are a product company, you could break yours by using your target segments or using your major product categories.

Your sales forecast needs to include a corresponding row for each sales row to cover the Cost of Goods Sold, also called the 'direct costs' – These show the expenses related to making your product or delivering your service. However, this should only include those expenses directly related to making your products, and not in any way including unrelated and other not regular business expenses such as rent expenses, insurance, salaries, and like.

Say, for restaurants, it means the cost of ingredients. And for a product company, it would be the cost of raw materials. Likewise, for a consulting business, it might be the paper costs, as well as presentation materials.

- **Personnel Plan**

How much you plan pm, paying your employees is basically what the personnel plan is all about.

For a small company, you may enlist in your personnel plan every position your company has, as well as how much each work will be paid each month.

Their personnel plan is usually broken down into functional groups such as "marketing" and "sales" for larger companies.

An "employee burden" should also be included in the personnel plan. – this refers to an employee's cost beyond salary, including payroll taxes, insurance, and all other necessary expenses that your company will incur every month to having such an employee on your payroll.

- **Income Statement or Profit or Loss Statement (P&L)**

The profit and loss or P&L, also known as Income Statement, is where numbers all come together as one to show if you are making a profit or incurring a loss. The P&L takes all data from your sales forecast, personnel plan, and the list of all your ongoing expenses concerning running your business.

The P&L should show in it the most important "bottom line" – where your expenses are being subtracted from your earnings to evaluate whether the business is making a profit or just potentially incurring losses while you grow.

A typical P&L is just a spreadsheet with the usual details as follows:

Sales or Income or Revenue

This comprises all revenue your business generated, usually from your sales forecast worksheet.

- **Cost of Goods Sold (COGS)**

And this refers to the total cost of selling your product, also called 'direct costs' in service-based businesses or the 'worth of sales

A promotion plan explains how you plan on communicating with your prospects and customers. At this point, make sure to consider that promotional programs that aren't profitable are hard to maintain in the

- **Gross Margin**

To get the figures for this, you need to subtract your COGS from your total sales. In most profit and loss statements, it is being shown as a percentage of total sales with the formula: (gross margin/sales= gross margin percentage)

- **Operating Expenses**

This comprises the list of your expenses concerning running your business, excluding the COGS you already discussed in detail. Costs such as taxes, depreciation, and repayment have to excluded here. Still, you need to include salaries, research, and development expenses, including marketing expenses and all others directly related to operating the business.

- **Total Operating Expenses**

This is simply the sum of all your operating expenses.

- **Operating Income**

This refers to your earnings before interest, taxes, depreciation, and repayment by subtracting your total operating expenses and COGS from your sales.

Interest, Taxes, Depreciation, and Repayment

Should list these below your operating income. If you have it, enlist appropriately.

Total Expenses

When you add your operating expenses together with interest, taxes, depreciation, and repayment altogether, these make up your total expenses.

- **Net Profit**

This comprises the all-important bottom line showing if you made a profit or incurred a loss at a specific month or year.

"THE RESILIENT ENTERPRISES"
Most Challenging 2021

- **Cash Flow Statement**

This statement will show you how much cash you have at any given time, commonly confused with the P&L statement, though a considerable difference between the two exists. The former is a statement that measures how well a company manages its cash position by keeping track of your cash flows. In contrast, the latter is one that calculates your profits and losses accordingly.

Put the difference between cash and profits. If you need to send a bill to your customer, it took 30 or 60 days to pay the bill. Thus, you don't have the bill right away, but you must have booked the sale in your P&L and shown a profit on the day you made the sale. Typically, a cash flow starts with the amount of cash you have on hand. Then, it will add money received through sales will be added. And subtracts cash paid out as pay bills, pay off loans, pay taxes, and the like. The remaining serves as your total cash flow, the formula being: cash in minus cash out equals ending cash (cash in − cash out + ending cash).

This will cue you whenever you might be running low on cash and when will the best time to buy new equipment be. Above all, it will guide you to decide how much money you should borrow to grow the company more. Thus, it is your guide to figure out low cash points and consider bringing in additional cash.

- **Balance Sheet**

This sheet provides an overview of a company's financial health. And this is typically the final financial statement most businesses need to create as part of their business plans. The company's assets, liabilities, including the owner's equity, are all shown here. And, subtracting the company's liabilities from its assets gives the company's net worth.

- **Use of Funds**

How you plan on using your investor's cash should be discussed here if you are raising money from investors.

It may not be as detailed as showing where every last centavo will go, though. What matters is showing the significant areas where will spend the investors' fund it could be on marketing expenses, perhaps research and development, sales, or might as well on purchasing inventory.

1. Register web domains and trademarks

These two things are the images of your business. It's true that without a digital presence, we can't go further in this digital world we currently live in. thus, every businessman should ensure the registration of its business' website domain, as well as its trademark. I would also recommend that every entrepreneur do this research together before registering your business because basically, you can plan your business name and available web domains first. As we go further living in the digital world, websites for companies have become more and more crucial as having none would mean your business is losing many opportunities found online. Through a website, can do lots of marketing strategies that could play an essential role in your business to grow. Apart from the marketing opportunities, your business could have from having a website.

A website publishes credibility for a business. Besides being able to market your business through a website, it also shows a map and directions to the company's shops or offices to

"THE RESILIENT ENTERPRISES"
Most Challenging 2021

easily find their locations. One important thing is that at least you have the scope to represent your customers on why they should trust you, as well as the testimonials and facts to back it up.

As time goes by, people are becoming busier, but because of the advancement in technology, people are becoming smart too. So, since they don't have that much time physically visiting the shop, they search for everything on the internet instead. Everything about the brand, features, price, size, colours, and all other relevant information: aside from credibility, offering good services or products can also boost your business through word-of-mouth. Thus, a website can give your business credibility and a positive impression that your company is more prominent and successful. Moreover, a website has a far more extensive reach than any other form of advertising. It will serve as the centre of your company's online presence. You can advertise it around all existing social networking sites and forums, including through pay-per-click advertising programs, which is one most important things to consider using a website. Because establishing an online presence through the use of a website, your company's size does not matter. Thus, the use of the website becomes more important for small businesses than bigger ones. Because of the availability and accessibility of the website 24/7, customers and potential customers opt to visit at any time to get more information about your business and to check product availability or check out some upcoming new products. This is more convenient than personally visiting the shop, which could be a burden for customers living far from your physical store's location. Although there are lots of marketing strategies you may use to advertise your business, many businesses have proven online marketing strategies using them to be more

"THE RESILIENT ENTERPRISES"
Most Challenging 2021

effective. The question of which one you should use depends on the type of business you are in. overall, a website establishes your business. Almost all customers expect every business to have an online presence.

A well designed, informative, and updated website will add credibility to your business and strengthen your product is the key to success in the modern marketplace, which is essential to every aspect of your company's marketing strategy. Every communication type, a piece of content or advertisement, and every bit of information you display online will surely drive your consumer back to your website for more. It indeed serves as the backbone of your online presence.

Now, why do you think trademark registration is essential? Let's find out.

Trademark registration enables you to show and claim that you have proof of ownership over your product/brand, and this is something that you can offer to the public. It simply means having a registered trademark gives you the right to use it as you deem fit without having to worry about legal consequences. With that, you are also allowed to stop anyone else illegally using it on your behalf.

Aside from those mentioned above, what is the function of a trademark? One of the trademark's essential functions is identifying the source or origin of products or services exclusively, so a brand indicates source or serves as a badge of origin. It merely means that a trademark serves as an identity or it identifies an entity as the source of goods and services.

2. Form your website:

After registration your web domain and your company as a whole, you should also select your preferred hosting package in preparation for the launching of your website. You can again hire a professional developer for this matter to do it for you efficiently. Moreover, when planning your website, I would recommend you do some research about similar websites, which is not only limited to your county, you can explore a broader range from all over the globe. Likewise, you may research business web site names, user-friendly interfaces, website themes with suitable colours, website features, and above all, website contents.

Now, what is an organizational structure? This system outlines how certain activities are directed to achieve an organization's goals, which includes certain activities such as rules, roles, and individual responsibilities.

It also determines the flow of information between all levels within the company. In a centralized structure, decisions flow from top-down, whereas in a decentralized system, decision-making power is distributedg among various groups within the organization. It allows companies to remain efficient and focused.

Thus, businesses of the same shape and sizes use organizational structures heavily.

A successful organizational structure explains each employee's job and further shows how it fits the overall system. Simply put, the organizational structure lays out who does what to meet its overall goals. This structuring provides an organization with a visual representation of how it has shaped

"THE RESILIENT ENTERPRISES"
Most Challenging 2021

and how it can best achieve its goals. An organizational structure is usually illustrating in some chart or diagram like a pyramid. The organization's most potent sits on the top while those with little power are at the bottom.

Key Takeaways:

A. An organizational structure shows a rough draft of how certain activities are direct to achieve the goals of the organization

B. A successful organizational structure defines each employee's job and how it fits within the overall system.

3. Implement a business structure:

You have to think skillfully when starting your own business. When processing your business structure, consider the following steps:

1. Prepare organized job descriptions;
2. Analyse current staff;
3. Make a description of job positions to be added;
4. Lastly, create an organizational chart.

4. Ensure that you can grow this business:

When you think about your business as a resilient entrepreneur, you will see your business from an advanced perspective. Being resilient, you can optimize how history is being shaped, how the current situation is doing, and what the future holds. And research is the only critical factor of this phase. Suppose you could analyse your business' proper costing and ensure efficient market awareness. In that case, you could at least set a goal within a specific duration of time on how much you can gain profits from the business. While it is important always to think positively, risk analysis should be your utmost priority in your industry.

5. Open a business bank account:

Business banking is not only a need but mandatory in every business. In the modern world we live, one can no longer survive in a business without banking. Even for average individuals, banking became a necessity for a day-to-day transaction.

You should open a business bank account immediately after your business has a registration or as soon as it begins to spend or accept money.

However, a sole partnership isn't legally required to open a business bank account. Still, it should get one anyway because a business bank account is a prerequisite in obtaining business loans, the reason being that the lenders won't approve your business loans unless funds can be deposit into a business bank account.

Furthermore, a business bank account is a must if you want to accept a credit card for your services or merchandise. Also, if you have an e-commerce, you'll surely need a business bank account to accept payments through your point-of-sale system.

Advantages of owning a business Bank Account

A business bank account makes it easier for you to manage your financials and protect your assets in case of a lawsuit.

- Clean Financial Records

It is recommending for every business person to open a business bank account because it lessens the possibilities of having issues or problems caused by mixing up personal savings and business finances. Thus, opening a business account can help you separate business from personal expenses, which results in the more effective management of your business cash flow through a clear overview of spending and costs.

Separating personal bank account from your business bank account will surely help you organize and manage well, especially in terms of year-end deductions such as taxes, and it will give you a clear audit trail.

6. Arrange business insurance:

At the onset of your business, this is not a need. But when you begin to expand and grow your business more prominent, you should go for it. That is to give your business assurance and protective armours in whatever assets you have in your business.

Business insurance can also help pay the costs of property damages. Some businesses buy multiple coverages and seldom combine them in one policy to ensure protection against specific risks unique to them.

7. Register for taxes:

This is one of the most important things to consider when starting your own business. Always make sure to open a tax file or a tax account in your own country. You can discuss this matter with your business consultant and get advice about this concern.

8. Create social network accounts:

Considering the modern world with advanced technology, Facebook, Instagram, Twitter, and Google business pages have become an indispensable part of owning a business, ensuring efficient business awareness. Creating a Facebook account and page for your business is ideal. And, gaining more followers can be useful for you to have an effective marketing channel using Facebook's advertising feature, which has been on the rise in business marketing recently.

Create Brand Recognition

Every business owner's ultimate goal should be to gain brand recognition. It's mainly because consumers surely patronize brands they recognize. The good thing is that social media allows us to build and establish a brand quickly.

Social media indeed has that great advantage over traditional media because it can just lay down your brand in front of the people easily.

Connect with your audience through Social Listening

Social listening is keeping up with the social conversations and topics to understand the current trend these audiences are following and to get information about what is essential for the market now. Moreover, you will also know what they are struggling with, guiding you by creating content to address those pain points.

"THE RESILIENT ENTERPRISES"

Most Challenging 2021

Tell Your Brand Story

Social media is an effective way to share your brand's mission and share relevant stories about it. Compelling stories can have a significant impact on your brand's image.

Build Customer Loyalty

Do you know that 55% of your customers are likely to be loyal to your business? That means they are likely to choose you over your competition.

9. Select effective and right employees:

As discussed above, in implementing a business structure, we always need to keep an eye on our employees. We have to analyse how productive they are comprehensively and the impact they make on the business. We can always groom our employees by requiring them some relevant training, especially motivational ones, to keep their focus aligned with their personal growth goals. Pieces of training concerning proper work ethics are also ideal for guiding them with the company's standards in performing their respective tasks while keeping up with the traditional working ethics. Moreover, technical training, especially those helpful in properly doing your business, would be precious. Like training on customer service, sales, and marketing, these could enhance your employees' skills in these specific areas that can be treated as an advancement to pursue your business's goals effectively.

Hiring the 'right' person

Hiring the wrong person will cost you more than just money. Thus, in every business hiring the right person is not only essential; it is an investment. To ensure that the company isn't losing any cent, hire the right person from the front desk to executive offices.

Time

While managing people takes time, dealing with a poor performance alone can take up to 70% more time than a good performance.

Having the right people can keep your focus on running your business right rather than worry too much about whether your workforce is doing the job the right way, which is such a waste of time.

Customer Service

Without the right people in your customer service role, better yet, tell your customers to engage your competition's services instead.

By hiring the right person, you are more likely to cultivate the market's best customer service experience.

Business Growth

Hiring the right people for your business means you won't be needing to hire more as your company grows; why? Because those interested candidates who invested in your company will be up to increasing their roles in your company matures.

10. Be technology-oriented:

Nowadays, a business can't be efficient without technology. The use of technology plays a massive role in every company's dealings, as discussed more intensively in the previous chapters on how the business world embraced the digital age. Let's just simply talk about the basics: social media platforms, websites, Google, and Microsoft packages. Imagine your business without them. It is just like you without Facebook. And these are all essential parts from the onset of your business.

11. Select efficient business digital platforms:

In selling products or offering services, you can use persuasive and highly efficient digital media to maintain a profitable business on track. Likewise, Microsoft excel or QuickBooks, and other similar professional digital platforms are highly advisable for accounting and auditing tasks, depending on the nature and number of workloads and the budget you have.

12. Keep focused on current and future business trends:

A resilient businessman always keeps an eye on the business environment's progress and development. It's a must for you to be ready if relevant changes occur, which might seriously affect your business. Keeping yourself updated on the current location and market trends could prepare you for what adjustments you need to make for your business to cope with future trends.

Following the guide, as mentioned above, will surely keep you on the perfect track with your business start-ups.

In addition to these, the following are also some critical areas to consider as you move forward:

"THE RESILIENT ENTERPRISES"
Most Challenging 2021

- **Start simple and small** –

Always make sure not to complicate your concepts and all the ideas you have in mind. It will be safer for you to start small and have a narrow focus. As the saying goes, "simplicity is best." Because the more complicated your idea becomes, the more expensive, it will get you to start, impractical.

- **Focus on niches** –

Put your focus on your target market instead of focusing a lot on your product. Many start-ups are falling short in this area. Some tend to give more attention to their products that they failed to consider their target market, which is a common mistake for many business people who are just starting. Anyone can come up with an extraordinarily innovative product. But you will surely not go anywhere if there isn't a concrete market for it. Instead of focusing too much on the product to drive sales, focus on developing a product, people are willing to buy. In short, know your market.

- **Never underestimate** cost –

Chances are, you're going to be overspending a lot when you are just starting. You must always be prepared for the worst and make sure to overestimate costs; never do otherwise.

- **Create your reliable support team** –

"No man is an island," as they say. In business, it's also the case. You can't effectively run a business, especially during the start-up, without your so-called turn-to people. Creating a team to support doesn't always mean they should be your business partners nor your start-up employees. Sometimes they are just

"THE RESILIENT ENTERPRISES"
Most Challenging 2021

your family, your circle of real friends you can consider your reliable support team. Like we always say, change is constant. So, challenges and obstacles are still inevitable. So, having your support team fall back on during your tough times can surely help you fuel up to have all the courage to move forward.

- **Always revisit your business idea –**

Finding out that your product's market exists just your head start. It doesn't stop there. Make sure to always review your business idea. As such, I never skip market research. Find out more about how the niche you are heading to works. Reassess your target market's strengths and weaknesses. Learn more about your audience's interest boosters. Perhaps, try to find how you could trigger a hype.

- **Measure your commitment –**

Perhaps ask yourself these questions: "are you ready to start a business?" "How ready?" – saying you are all set and ready doesn't only mean you are prepared financially. Along with your start-up, everything around will undoubtedly require you some emotions. Thus, saying you are now ready to start hitting the ground should also mean you are ready emotionally. Never forget that in running a business, time is also an investment. You will compromise your relationship with some people, which is essential. Thus, you should also be sure to be emotionally-ready not to compromise your business management as your business progresses. Next chapter, we'll talk more about business start-up essentials. Keep going.

"THE RESILIENT ENTERPRISES"

Most Challenging 2021

Chapter 6

"The Business Start-up Essentials"

Now that we have learned about the typical hustle and grinds of business start-ups, in this chapter, we'll talk about the essentials things every business person shouldn't miss in starting up a business.

Business Planning

A business plan contains technical aspects of business start-ups, such as typical goal-setting and organized plans in achieving it. It includes a written scheme for the company from the marketing aspect to its financial feature, and the operational angle, all written technically according to the company's guide.

Every start-up person in business commits common mistakes because they fail to plan; perhaps they don't take time to plan. Because some are just too consumed by the concepts, they tend to disregard the idea of proper planning. When disruptions happen and the need to set back occurs, no reliable document is there to guide them to decide, as they failed to make the required business plan beforehand. Thus, tendencies to fail at the onset are high.

In this book, we will guide you step-by-step on how to make your business plan properly. Check it out below.

Following is the proper process of Business Planning:

"THE RESILIENT ENTERPRISES"
Most Challenging 2021

1st step: Set Objectives: in this step, you need to identify the goals you want to achieve. Decide what you're going to do.

2nd step: Strategy Formulation: this step simply answers the question: **"how do you plan to do it?"** – this is closely intertwined with step 1 because you need to have goals first before you can formulate strategies on how to achieve them.

3rd step: Make proper organization: This step is explained by answering the question, **"who will make it?"** Thus, after setting up goals and formulating strategies. Here, you need to arrange the people required to perform the process to achieve your goals effectively. So, you need to pick the right people to accomplish your objectives efficiently.

4th step: Implement: implementation is the most crucial part, though. For even if you have all the business plans in the world, if you don't take action, nothing will happen; you won't go anywhere, either. A business plan is just a business plan until it is putting into action. You also need to make proper monitoring of your action plans' steps to keep you progressing on the right track. –- it means, be very careful in moving forward. Are you hitting your desired result? If not, something is wrong with your implementation. Revisit them.

Market Analysis

One essential feature of a Business Plan is Market Analysis. There can't be a concrete business plan without it. Because a Market Analysis is simply the appropriate and comprehensive evaluation of your target market as a whole following your business' features. It is a thorough examination of the market through a quantitative and qualitative study to gather relevant market information useful for your business.

This may include size of your target market, market segmentation, their buying patterns, your possible competitors, the economic environment, as well as the regulations, If there's any, such as the barriers to entry and the like.

But how is Market Analysis being done, and what it is? let me answer first, for the second question: objectives of the Market Analysis section in a business plan is to assure your investors that you got the right market and that you know them accurate in detail, which will further guarantee them the sustainability and feasibility of your business.

Capital Investment

So, what's a capital investment? And what is it for, In business, capital investment has two usages? First, capital investment refers to the money invested in a business to cover such a business's day-to-day operating expenses. Secondly, capital investment's widespread usage is to acquire fixed assets such as land, machinery, or buildings.

Following are some primary and common reasons why a business makes capital investments:

First and foremost is to acquire additional capital assets for expansion purposes, which will enable the business to increase unit production, for example. And to create new products or add value. Secondly, to take advantage of technological advancements in machinery and equipment, which enables the business to increase efficiency and reduce costs. Lastly, to advance and replace existing assets that have already depreciated, such as delivery vehicles, computers, laptops, etc., are examples of assets that depreciate fast.

Marketing

Marketing is a process following this pattern: creating à communicating à delivering -à and exchanging offers that have values for customers, clients, partners, and society at large.

Simply, it's a course in the business world taken by entrepreneurs and businssmens for the same goal: monetizing the business by way of producing something of value with the end goal of offering the same to people who will probably need them for a cost and who are likewise willing and can afford to pay for them. They may be but are not limited to, the customers, clients, partners, and society

Types of Marketing

- **Influencer Marketing**

Per ANA, influencer marketing focuses on leveraging individuals with potential influence over a possible group of buyers, and by orienting marketing activities around these individuals to drive,]'

In influencer marketing, a brand compensates influencers such as celebrities, customer advocates, employees, etc., to get the word out on their behalf.

- **Relationship Marketing**

These refer to the marketing strategy of segmenting consumers to build loyalty. It influences database marketing, behavioural advertising to target consumers precisely and creates loyalty programs.

"THE RESILIENT ENTERPRISES"

Most Challenging 2021

The Marketing Strategies

The two (2) main types of marketing strategy are as follows:

Business to business (B2B) marketing: as its name suggests, B2B marketing refers to marketing products or services to other businesses or organizations. It holds several differences from B2C marketing, which later you will learn more in detail. On a more comprehensive view, B2B marketing contents appear to be more informational and straightforward than B2C. Generally, a business purchase is grounded more on its impact on its revenue as a whole. Thus, the buying in B2B is being made to consider its probable impact to achieve outstanding ROI fully. So, B2B marketing is for companies that sell to other companies as their prospects. And, this can come in many structures such as, but not limited to, software-as-a-service or the so-called SAAS, subscriptions, security solutions, tools, accessories, office supplies, and the like, you can name all of them! As such, B2B marketing campaigns are aimed at individuals with direct control or authority in purchasing decisions, with the potential ROI being their primary consideration.

Being that, competition for customers, in this case, is too high. Thus, building a strong and steady B2B marketing strategy with a guaranteed appropriate result requires in-depth planning, proper execution, and competent management.

To help you achieve that, the following are B2B marketing's best practices you may use as a guide:

- **Be human:** so, yes! You are selling to a company, but this doesn't mean you are marketing to a business establishment or a non-tangible being, no! of course.

"THE RESILIENT ENTERPRISES"
Most Challenging 2021

While you are selling to a company as a whole, that could also mean you are trying to reach actual people within that specific company. Given that, don't just learn about the company you are trying to pursue. You should also learn about the people within them and make sure your marketing is directly speaking to them, don't be too vague.

- **Focus on targeting:** take the time to define and segment your target audience efficiently. Otherwise, you will be wasting time and effort. Yes, because every extensive campaign indeed leads to wasted time and effort spent. Why? Because while doing so, you are undeniably serving content and ads to people who might be either uninterested or unable to influence buying decisions. To avoid this situation, you should always create content and messaging that speaks directly to a specific group of people you wanted to see.

- **Keep Context in Mind:** personalization and significance are essential in B2B marketing. Here, you would want to speak the language of your customers. But that isn't always enough. You also want to deliver contents and advertisements that fit practically with where they are being viewed. For example, shorter videos with quick catches can perform more effectively on social media feeds, while longer videos will probably perform better on YouTube. To sum it up, B2B, although a business to business marketing, still you're speaking to humans, so don't stumble into a trap of being excessively formal.

- Furthermore, genuinely effective B2B marketing is conventional, targeted, and contextually relevant. The easiest way to explain B2B marketing is that B2B transactions take more consideration, involves more people, especially ones in authority. It requires more decision-makers because B2B target clients need to prove a potential return-on-investment for their purchase as it's their utmost consideration above all.

Business to Customer (B2C) marketing: from its name itself Business-to-consumer, it's the campaigns and strategies in which a company promotes its products and services intended to individual people: so, it's merely creating, advertising, and selling products for customers use. So, when you are marketing to a consumer, your focus should be on the product's benefits. Unlike B2B clients, here, the consumer's decision is more sensitive. Consumers are also different, so some of them would demand various distribution channels for convenience. Thus, the tendency is, consumers are less likely interested in an extensively lengthy marketing message and want straight-to-the-point content. B2C consumers don't exert efforts to understand the benefits they could get from your products or services. Instead, it should be you who should exert efforts to point out to them clearly and directly those benefits they want to hear. With this, your marketing message should be simple and easy to understand, not too broad and complicated. Unlike in B2B as well, B2C consumers have a shorter purchasing process. They can purchase within a few days, even within a few minutes, since they are not very concerned about the possible ROI they could get. Hence, the most effective B2C marketing strategies should focus on the results and the benefits your product or service will bring.

Moreover, customers will want to hear more about how a product or service can help them personally. So, focus on the problem or issues and point how your product or service could solve them. Consider productivity software, for example. What the consumers would want to know is how the software is going to make their lives easier. And how would it sync with family members' phones and laptops, etc.? In this example, your customers are not looking for a return on their investment as they're only looking for software that could make their lives easier without being too complicated. Thus, businesses that focus on B2C marketing need to observe trends more closely, research their customer's purchase habits, and closely monitor their competitors' tactics. It is critical to know the challenges and understand how to break through all the noise to succeed.

The Marketing Concepts

Now, let us talk about marketing concepts. The following are the five marketing concepts. These philosophical concepts to the marketplace have guided and continue to conduct organizational activities. Check them out below:

- The Production Concept
- The Product Concept
- The Selling Concept
- The Marketing Concept
- The Social Marketing Concept

The Production Concept

This concept is considered the oldest of the ideas in business. It states that consumers will prefer products that are widely available and reasonably priced. Thus, Managers that focused on this concept concentrate majorly on achieving high production efficiency, low costs, and mass distribution, assuming that consumers are primarily interested in product availability and low prices. This orientation holds in developing countries where consumers are interested in obtaining the product than its features; hence, product availability will always be a priority. – which means, as the concept dictates, consumers are concerned about product availability above all other factors.

The Product Concept

This concept suggests that consumers will always go after those products that offer the most quality, performance, or innovative features. So, managers focusing on this concept concentrate on making superior products and improving them over time, assuming that buyers will always admire well-made products and appraise quality and performance. However, these managers are sometimes too focused on producing quality products that tend to forget the market's needs. As such, management might commit the "better-mousetrap" fallacy, holding a false belief that a superior product will automatically generate customers, believing that a better mousetrap will lead people to beat a path towards its door. Thus, while a businessman considers quality, never take 'what the market needs' out of the picture. Instead, it should be intertwined it with it to ensure success using this concept.

The Selling Concept

This is another standard business orientation that holds that consumers will not ordinarily buy enough of the selling company's products without any promotion efforts and aggressive selling. This means selling aggressively and putting efforts into promotions. Advertising is one factor to stimulate consumers to buy, and without them, there might be no reason for the consumers to buy. Thus, the need to persuade them to accept by practising the selling concept. Most firms practising this are those with a reasonable capacity to sell what they make rather than selling what the market needs.

The Marketing Concept

This is a philosophy that challenges the above business orientations. One key factor in achieving the selling company's organizational goals is to perform more effectively and efficiently in the market than the known competitors, especially in creating, delivering, and communicating customer value to its selected target customers. And this marketing concept emphasizes these four factors: target market, customer needs, integrated marketing, and profitability. To excel in the market using this concept is to put the utmost consideration of the above mentioned. That is, first, identifying your target market, know your target customer's needs, and then incorporate all competitive marketing strategies following the information you have, then evaluate the profitability of the business you are pursuing.

The 7P formula of Marketing

Earlier, we have discussed the concepts of marketing. This time, let us talk about the principles. The seven marketing principles are **product, price, promotion, place, packaging, positioning,** and **people.** The necessity to revisit these 7Ps continues as products, markets, customers, and needs change rapidly. You must continually review these seven 7Ps to make sure you are on track. Achieving the maximum results is possible for you in today's marketplace. Let us talk more about them:

"THE RESILIENT ENTERPRISES"

Most Challenging 2021

Product

This refers to what you are selling, including the features, advantages, and benefits buyers can have fun buying your products or services. When marketing your product, you need to think about the main features and benefits your customers want or need, including style, quality, repairs, and accessories, including, but not limited to, elements of your product that others do not have or didn't stand out from the crowd.

Price

This second and more crucial marketing formula is related to your products and services' pricing strategy and how it affects your customers. You should always include how much your customers are willing and ready to pay, including the profit margin needed to cover overheads, profit margins, payment methods, and other costs. You can also attract customers, and maintain your competitive edge, consider some possibilities for discounts and seasonal prices. Setting the right price for your products helps you maximize profits while maintaining a good relationship with your customers. Effective pricing can also help you avoid serious financial problems that may occur if your prices are too high or low Because if you charge too much, you may price yourself out of the market, while if you charge too low, may underpay you for your work.

Pricing your products and services does not have a stressful process. Just always consider the following:

- You are in business to make a profit, nothing more, nothing less;
- It is always easier to lower your prices than to raise them;

- Thorough research will help you establish the right price for your goods or services.;
- The right price is fair to your customers such that they are willing to pay for it and suitable for your business such that you can cover costs and make a profit.

Promotion

This next big P of marketing refers to the promotional activities used to make customers aware of products and services, including advertising, sales tactics, promotions, and direct marketing, which are generally referred to as marketing tactics. To be effective, you need to choose your promotional activities as marketing aims to stand out and be noticed and recognized. Good marketing keeps drawing your customer's attention to your products. Your defined, well-packaged, competitively-priced products and services are simply the foundation of your marketing. And, the newer you are in your chosen market, the harder it is for you to work your way to attract and retain new customers. Many of your marketing activities focus on communicating to customers the features and benefits of your competitors' products. Thus, always consider which promotional activities best meet your marketing needs.

Below are some types of promotional activities you might want to consider:

1. **Advertising:** you can advertise your product or service in newspapers, radio, television, magazines, outdoor signage, and online. Advertisement is an effective way of promoting your products and services to your target audience and is usually a paid promotion. When you advertise, you tell your prospective customers who you

are, where you are, and what you can do beneficial to them. A good advertisement should:

• Build your business image;

• Explain the benefits of your products and services.

• Increase awareness of new products and services before, when and after their launch.

• Generate interest in your target market, as well as a potential new target group;

• Encourage customers to request information about your business and provide options on how they can contact you.

• Increase customer demand and increase sales.

• Understand the wide range of advertising strategies that allow you to use the best for your business. You may also find that combinations of these strategies will give you the most substantial results.

2. Personal Selling or Marketing:

Significant face-to-face sales depend on good interpersonal and communication skills, excellent knowledge of products, services, and the ability to sell the product's benefits to potential customers. Good interpersonal and communication skills speak for sales skills as a whole. Because no matter how good your products or services are, your success still depends on your ability to sell them. Your business will either grow or

"THE RESILIENT ENTERPRISES"
Most Challenging 2021

fail depending on your product or service's success and how you convince your customers to buy it. Anyone can learn sales skills. And, no matter what you are selling, you can achieve great product sales by mastering a set of proven selling skills:

2.1 Confidence: As we have discussed above, confidence plays a crucial role in marketing. And, it's an understatement to say enthusiasm in marketing is essential. No! it is but a vast MUST. You can always know everything about your product and can possess significant experiences in the field. But, if potential buyers don't perceive you as confident, you will surely never succeed. Keep in mind that a large part of being successful in sales is developing sales confidence.

2.2 Relationship-Building: A human interaction, where the salesperson is generally interested in connecting with their customer or buyer, being concerned with establishing relationships with potential customers, and taking an interest in their world, can significantly improve the odds of securing a sale and keeping it. Customer. Long term.

2.3. Listen Always: Your client will tell you what he wants, so give him a chance to listen. Your role is to listen instead of being the one who talks all the time. Believe it! You will serve him better with the knowledge he shares with you. Then listen.

2.4 Persuasion - Of the many skills required to be a successful salesperson, being persuasive is probably one of the most important. Convincing others is part of your daily life. And if you're trying to get someone to change their mind or buy your product, persuading people effortlessly is essential to your success. It can be easy to oversimplify effective sales techniques, but to use this skill set, you must first that "persuasion" isn't just about talking. The art of persuasion is a mindset in its own right and mastering this skill requires preparation, practice, and persistence.

2.3. Product knowledge: Understanding your products' features allows you to present their benefits accurately and persuasively. Customers respond to active sales personnel passionate about their work and eager to share the benefits with them. So, product knowledge can mean more sales.

3. Publicity:

Another type of promotional activity is publicity, which is created by sending media releases to print and broadcast media, giving interviews to the press, and form word-of-mouth. Public relations or PR is the practice of managing and guiding your business's perceptions to attract new customers and strengthen existing customers' loyalty. Direct experiences can shape customers' perceptions, the actions, observations of others, and the statements you make in the media and marketplace. A well-planned PR strategy is a powerful tool for business. Unlike marketing and advertising, PR takes advantage of unpaid communication channels such as local and regional media, the internet, business networks, and community and customer relationships. Naturally, PR gathers more credibility than paid marketing efforts as a third party usually produces the results. PR involves communicating with your market to raise awareness of your business, build and manage your business's reputation and cultivate relationships with consumers. While marketing focuses on promoting actual products and services, PR focuses on promoting awareness, attitude, and behaviour changer.

4. Short-term sales promotions:

It's another type of promotional activity by marketing your product or services using coupons, competitions, and contests.

5. Direct marketing:

Lastly, another type of promotional activity involves sending letters, emails, pamphlets, and brochures to individual target clients, often allowed by personal selling or telemarketing.

You may use any combination of these methods to target your customers. And the right promotional mix will surely help you satisfy your customers' needs, improve your results, increase sales, and increase your ability to reach multiple customers within your target market.

Branding

Branding in the world of business is simply one way of identifying your business. It is through your brand that your customers recognize you and your business. A brand is more than just a logo as others perceive it. It is reflected in almost everything, from your customer service style, staff uniforms, business cards, and in all of your marketing materials and advertising. It has been said that your brand plan is more important than your business plan as a whole. People nowadays care more about your brand, basically about YOU and the WHO of your business, than your product. The reality nowadays is that customers would be more interested to know you first before buying your product. Thus, branding first before anything else. Successful branding starts with a good vision – it's the concept and collective ideas of what the brand should stand for. It's what it should symbolize or represent as a whole. And, along with the vision, also comes a mission. Such a combination of mission and vision should consist of the concrete attack that helps launch your brand. Also, a brand must have this alluring short message, which briefly explains everything that your company can do, which others can't.

Lastly, and the most critical feature of branding is its emotional aspect, which is how you and your products make your target customers feel. In every business, we should always care about customer's satisfaction; it should be the one that drives the business forward.

Maintaining Brand Personality

Maintaining Brand Personality is perhaps the most crucial part of marketing your business as it states what position you are in in the market and has lots of impact on who will buy your product. Without a strong and consistent brand personality, your business will have difficulty keeping up with its niche audience. When it comes to smaller businesses, brand personality isn't .merely important; it's everything! And the main reasons why you need to create a brand personality for your business are: first, it enables you to stand out from the crowd, it gets your business' message across just as how your favourite brand of clothes give you personal feelings of recognition and familiarity, warmth and comfort, which perhaps are the reasons you prefer such brand over another. For example, below are two well-known brands in the market:

a. Apple; and,
b. Microsoft.

"THE RESILIENT ENTERPRISES"

Most Challenging 2021

Apple is being loved because of its artistic, creative, and stylish features. At the same time, Microsoft has well known for its business-oriented features, versatility, quality, and high performance.

Going back to the times when watching a commercial of dancing silhouettes with iPod on TV has been mainstream. For sure, you have noticed improvements and the massive difference in brand personality between apple and Microsoft since then. Nowadays, with your graphic designer attached to his iMac, your accountant typing away from his PC laptop, you can see that the personality of each brand is the same as it was fifteen years ago, you can do graphic designs on a PC, and can use spreadsheets on a Mac, but these aren't the reasons why people choose them. Instead, your graphic designer was likely drawn by apple's creative personality. Likewise, your accountant was also lured to Microsoft's business-oriented nature. Your small business has to maintain its position in the market as well through its brand personality. Let's set another example. Say you own a pizza shop, and you make great artisan, brick-oven style pizza. But, one of your competitors holds a corporate pizza place. So, you mustn't lower your product's quality to make pizza as fast as the chain store can because that will change your brand personality. If you decide to start working as a corporate chain pizza place, you are opening up the market for another artisan pizza to take away your business. You must understand that you should focus on your business's strengths and opportunities for you to continue to be known as the place where you can go and get a great pizza made with extra care and a unique recipe. For example, when McDonald's starts selling pizza, people will see it as wildly out of place, and you should avoid committing the same mistakes.

"THE RESILIENT ENTERPRISES"

Most Challenging 2021

The following are the five (5) dimensions of brand personality called the 'Big Five' Personality Traits

The Big Five Personality Traits

Strategic Selling

Strategic selling, more than just selling strategically, means strategizing in selling by sincerely considering a customer's perspective. Strategic selling works by understanding your company's strategies, mission, and vision profoundly, and your distinctiveness, among others, then targeting high profile customers. It is not merely selling for a return of investment. Instead, it is more on addressing the buyer's concerns when making a sale to establish long-term relationships with the customer. Various strategic selling techniques are employed to enhance sales volume and build a lasting relationship with customers. Personal selling, after-sales service, maintaining contacts, and low pricing strategy are just some of the commonly used strategic selling techniques. Know more about them below:

Personal selling

It aims to build a good relationship between the buyer and seller to enable the buyer to buy an item without feeling pressured or forced. A good relationship between the seller and the buyer is developed effectively when the seller is more concerned about meeting the customer's needs rather than just pursuing a successful sale. Personal selling addresses the buyer's preferences and focuses significantly on the product's powerful features being offered. Furthermore, the seller gives an honest and transparent response to the customer's objections. Through this approach, it can develop a lasting strategic relationship

After-sales Service

This refers to the additional services the seller offers to the buyer after they have purchased a product. These services include but are not limited to deliveries, item installations, and warranty services to enhance convenience and quality experience to help bolster a positive image for the company.

Maintaining Contacts

It's merely keeping in touch with the buyer to confirm whether the item purchased is doing well or if the buyer needs further assistance about it.

Low pricing strategy

This is the strategy commonly used by businesses that are just starting. The strategy offers comparatively low initial prices on specific products to stimulate unsolicited demand and gain market share.

Besides, Strategic Selling depends on what you are going to sell, goods, or services. You have to consider "place" – it means the environment, opportunity, situation, and customer psychology matters. But not only that. Aside from place, "right time" or the perfect time is also significant. – it means you have to make sense of your target customer's purchasing power. Customer psychology matters, as well. A customer wants and needs a business climate. Above all, the "right people" are our utmost consideration – it means, when we cater for our product or services and implement a strategy, we should always analyze who the people capable of buying this are. We should comprehensively identify who has the purchasing power to buy this, who are those who can afford this, and who are those who need this. – this refers to our target segment. If you put utmost considerations on these critical factors, then you are hitting the win for sure.

Overall, strategic selling can be a bit complicated and seldom challenging to master. But, in reality, can simplify its comprehensive course into three essential words. And these words are WALK, TALK, NOTE. – and, what are these all about, How are these related to developing strategic selling skills? Keep reading.

WALK. TALK. NOTE.

In developing your business skills, especially in this essential skill in selling, strategic selling, while some get satisfied already with the information they get from the internet, don't be one. Because the real score is, not all information we get from our research on Google is happening in the real world. Some of them are merely concepts and might not even actually happening. And the best way to get the actual scenarios happening around us is to master the concept of WALK, TALK, NOTE. This concept will give you the real picture of how a resilient entrepreneur acquires his advanced strategic selling skills. Let's start with the **WALK** – perhaps, it's the most effective way to obtain the relevant information you need to advance in the strategies you use for your business, especially in competing in the market. Walk connotes its literal meaning, that when you are walking anywhere, be very vigilant as a resilient entrepreneur. This means, observe around with a

"THE RESILIENT ENTERPRISES"

Most Challenging 2021

more comprehensive perspective and try to analyse every information you get. For example, digital advertising, holdings, billboards, architectural buildings, window appearances of the outlets, shopping malls, branding themes, promotions, posters, and the like, everything you can see as you walk might be useful for your business. Above all, as you continue walking, make practical observations of every individual's behaviour you come across, be it a seller, a buyer, or both. These observations from your analysis from actual cases are undoubtedly more reliable than ones you get from Google, which are purely hypothetical. Secondly, we have the TALK. – simply put, one can never come across somebody without having at least a small talk. Every person we meet, business-oriented or not, indeed adds to the analysis we create by merely talking and exchanging thoughts can gather more relevant information, be it solicited or voluntarily given; it's a case-to-case basis. But either way, both are useful. Like, we might come across a customer in a mall complaining about a specific product he bought. We could get simple information such as likes, dislikes, tastes, preferences, and the like through the complaints. Through this information we get as we talk with people we meet on our walk, we slowly put together the puzzle we need to solve on 'what the market needs?' and all other questions pertinent to sales. Lastly, we have **noted** – and, I must say, it's the most important in this concept. It just sums up everything from a walk and talk. It means all information you get as you walk and talk. It is a MUST to note all of them. At all times, on any occasion, always keep a note. A resilient entrepreneur keeps a message of important information, business cards, relevant references, locations, and important places, especially highly influential people's records. – if you get

"THE RESILIENT ENTERPRISES"
Most Challenging 2021

yourself familiar with this simple method of improving yourself in strategic selling, your analytical knowledge will be more exposed.

"THE RESILIENT ENTERPRISES"

Most Challenging 2021

Chapter 7

"Sales Master"

With the advanced technology, we currently have, pursuing sales shall be at its advanced level too. – before jumping into your first-ever sales experience, make sure to learn the basics first. Keep in mind that every sales master was once a beginner like you. Needless to say, that in every dealing we have, learning the fundamentals is but a MUST. Thus, on our next subtopic discussion, let us talk about the basics of a seller.

Basics of a Seller

So, what do you think are the necessary qualities of a seller? Let us check them one by one if you have them.

Following are the essential qualities of a good salesperson:

1. Confidence.

Every seller possesses the required amount of confidence to achieve outstanding and promising deals in sales. Confidence, mostly for beginners, play a considerable role in the world of selling. Because selling is nothing but 60% of listening and 40% talking—the composition should be like this, nothing less. With the only 40% talking requirement, expect to fail if you don't possess the desired level of confidence every entrepreneur needs. To achieve being a sales master, consider developing your confidence level, keeping the ability to sell with confidence, and confidently deliver your answer to your customer's objections in case you need to.

2. Ability to listen.

A good salesperson is a good listener, as they say. The ability to listen is one of the most important points of being a good salesperson. In selling, our end goal should always be 'to satisfy our client's needs' and not the other way around. Thus, we should know what the client wants or needs. One way to achieve that is by listening to them attentively. This supports those who claim that 'the better the seller's listening ability is, the better the sales conversation will be,' subsequently resulting in a successful sales negotiation.

3. Empathy.

A good salesperson is one who is empathetic. An empathetic salesperson knows accurately how to understand what their customers feel by getting inside their customer's shoes. With that, they know precisely just how to sell the product or the service the most effective by trying to be empathetic and sharing the same point of view with the customer. in fact, it is the most effective way of anticipating what a customer needs. We know for a fact that people buy from the people they trust. And empathy builds trust. since it is an emotional intelligence skill every salesperson must-have. As it defines, it is the ability to understand share the feelings of another by putting yourself in their shoes. It is the power to understand your clients' sentiments without having them explicitly state it to you. If you think you don't have this kind of skill, then it's time for you to start developing your empathetic selling skills, techniques, and strategies now. – As the saying goes, "you will never really understand a person until you consider things from his point of view. And that exactly what the art of empathizing is.

4. Competitiveness.

Another essential quality of a good salesperson is competitiveness. And being competitive in the world of selling is a combination of the following elements: proper mindset, competition, and accurate positioning. Let us talk about it more deeply.

1. Proper mindset. Successful deals and competitive selling all start with your mindset. Your mindset should be moulded appropriately with the right motivation to feel empowered. A good mindset shouldn't be driven by your desired income, but rather by your customer's satisfaction; it should always be your priority. And business challenges eventually lead to personal achievements. It's like you see sales as a game to play and something to have fun with to win.

2. Competition. Competition doesn't always really mean you have to keep comparing yourself to others and strive to be better against all of them. Sometimes it simply means getting to know your competitors in the market and being knowledgeable about what they offer that you don't. It is for you to develop a unique and different solution to address your competitiveness concerns to survive the competition effectively.

"THE RESILIENT ENTERPRISES"

Most Challenging 2021

The Art of Persuasion

Now that you have all the basics of being a seller, you have read in the previous sub-chapter. It is time for you to explore more about how to be effective in selling. This chapter will talk about the secret of every top seller's practice, 'the Art of persuasion.' How effective is persuasive selling? And, what do you think are the principles behind the art of persuasion? Let's find out.

In selling, either goods or services, keep in mind that one thing you need to achieve. – it's making your prospective buyers believe in the same thing. And that's where persuasion works. In the context of business, persuasion is all about building trust and a good relationship with your customer. Your end goal should be to establish an irresistible image of your product that becomes indispensable to your prospects. You should present your products how your prospects cannot say "NO" to, just like a painkiller they cannot live without. First, know their problems. Connect your product to such a problem, convince the prospect that your product can solve it and that it is the best option to resolve the issues they currently have. Just make sure to use the right words in persuading; play it smart. Following are the principles in persuasion cited by Robert Cialdini, a Psychology professor who conceptualized the following named Cialdini's principles of persuasion:

"THE RESILIENT ENTERPRISES"

Most Challenging 2021

Cialdini's Principles of persuasion

1. Reciprocity –

This is what Oprah Winfrey said, "life is a reciprocal exchange; you have to give back." Hence, Cialdini's first principle suggests that humans tend to act the way they have been treated. This means that what you showed to your potential prospect reflects the results you will get. If you showed them friendly gestures while trying to persuade them, they would also respond the same by doing something in return, which can be anything from a sale or something you value. Thus, the kinder you treat and deal with your clients, the happier they get, which can be converting into sales. Indirectly helping you make more sales, and that's how the law of reciprocity works in persuasion. The key is merely helping your client get the best satisfaction they could have by helping them overcome their problems with your product. Give and take, that's the first principle in persuasion, according to Cialdini.

2. Scarcity –

Another principle of persuasion we should discuss.

"Only one stock left" – how do you usually react when you see this in your favourite online store? Don't you cram and proceed to check out immediately? That explains the principle of scarcity in persuasion. This principle states that consumers tend to panic-buy when they see a possible shortage of a particular good, especially ones they need or want at a specific time. And it is considered a factor that triggers action And is the claim to be the best way to persuade potential buyers to purchase. This supports the idea that products are more valued when they are limited. According to Cialdini, scarcity is some kind of selling strategy that indirectly compels people to buy. This explains why some stores would display how many stocks per particular item are left. This is to stimulate faster action from potential prospects. It is one of the best ways to persuade people to buy.

3. Authority:

How do you usually react to hearing your boss' voice? It's something like trying to impose superiority. You seem to approve without any second thought to what he is saying, and you accede immediately. − this explains the principle of authority, which states that people tend to lend an ear to an authoritative voice. − it means people trust a person who is known to be knowledgeable in that particular field and has enough experience in it − as such, he has the authority to be listened to,

When you are unsure about buying a particular product, don't you usually search for an opinion from a person with authority? This explains why many companies use celebrities with authority over a specific field when advertising their products. Please note that it is not enough that a person helping you promote famously or has influence. The authority should always be there.

Assurance is the keyword there. Meaning, consumers want proof. Thus, when they see trusted people or a person with authority marketing for a specific product, that assures them that it is a good investment to purchase such product.

4. Consistency:

Another principle of persuasion is consistency. You can never go wrong with consistency. For a powerful sales result, you should create a consistent sales cycle because no matter what you do, people will surely notice if you are committed to dealing with them or not. People will always expect consistency, not only in dealing with prospects in a business. Say, in courting your ideal girl. She will surely expect consistency because she'll never how serious you are pursuing her without it. – the same holds in business. Show your prospects consistency, and they will surely do the same, also applying the law of reciprocity at the same time.

5. Liking:

In most cases, if not always, there are possibilities when you tend to be influenced by people whom you like and trust. This explains Cialdini's principle in persuasion, liking. It suggests that you need to be the person they will like, trust and trust first to persuade a person. First, you need to be presentable when you meet them. Assure them that you are there to help. Make genuine praise to establish a real and healthy relationship as well. Make it easier and comfortable for them to feel a connection with you. Being honest is also very important. Ensure them you are not only there for the sales.

6. Consensus:

This refers to social proof; nowadays, this becomes one of the most potent persuasive selling techniques. It is to give your potential buyers assurance that your product is trusted and used by others. – this is what the principle of consensus is all about. You might have wondered why some advertisements show that 88% of the world uses this.

Chapter 8

"Mevin's Consumer's Grade Approach"

As you go along with your business start-up, it will never be enough to have all your necessities ready then you can start. Because, even if you have all the unique, extraordinary, champion products, if you don't understand the people in your target market you are going to deal with, chances are, you will not achieve your desired results. What does it mean? It means that it will be better to get to know and understand your target audiences and your ideal customers. You are expecting to know this: Being a resilient entrepreneur is the discussion in this chapter. For the first time, in this book, I will introduce my market segmentation model, which I named **Mevin's Consumer's Grade Approach**. – this concept will help you understand your target audiences and who should be your ideal customers. After reading the entire model, it will help you identify the right market for your product or service, which will help you create your marketing strategies more effectively. And, Mevin's Consumer's Approach is a professional consumers' grade approach categorized into five grades: (on the road, above the road, sky, cloud, above the cloud.) and what are these? Let us talk more about it below:

"THE RESILIENT ENTERPRISES"

Most Challenging 2021

- **On the road:**

This is the first category of the concept of Mevin's Consumer's Approach to mean the very poor people, as its name suggests 'on the road,' they are ones we see on the road, homeless people, refugees, and the like. These people survive from donations as they don't have their daily income. Perhaps most of them rely on the government's support; some might be living in refugee camps only if not in an unknown land. These people don't have a single property, not even a bank account. Even proper meals they barely have. No clothes as the case usually. They rely on free medical assistance for the illnesses they suffer. They accept free education. In conclusion, these people under this category have little needs due to poverty.

- **Above the road:**

Next category of this consumer's approach, is still falling under poor people. But, unlike 'on the road,' these people have a daily income at least. It may be difficult for them, but they can somehow find ways to earn something. They don't depend on any donations; they eat what they have to eat, though. On the other hand, they have Minor consumption behaviour. They dress in low-quality clothes, and they buy the cheapest ones. They even need free medical assistance. Some of them might have bank accounts, but the funds in it aren't good enough. These people can't afford a nice dinner for the whole family, and they even need and accept free education. As such, they have limited needs.

- **Sky:**

This category is considered the most fluctuating layer globally under this consumer's concept, yet it is believed that most

"THE RESILIENT ENTERPRISES"
Most Challenging 2021

people live under this group. This grade represents the middle-income holders. They have fixed income; some might have many sources of revenue. They have some sort of vehicle with leasing or credit facility, and they have bank accounts; some might have credit cards. These people have good loan credibility. As such, some might have bank loans. There is competent consumer behaviour under this class, though, depending on particular occasions and gaining income. Most of them have properties of their own, insurance facilities even. They have enough funds to sustain their medications. Hence, they don't rely on any forms of free or donations. However, most of them might have just relied on their credit limits and loan availabilities to come up with their status. They have needs and wants. However, some accept free educations still. But some spend on their education expenses.

- **Cloud:**

This category has everything since they are group as rich people, but not the wealthy ones. They have properties; some might have more than one. These people have vehicles, one or more houses, more than enough bank funds, fixed investment deposits, shares, stocks, and run their businesses. Overall, they are financially stable. That's why they refuse free medical assistance with fewer facilities. Instead, they spend much on medications as they can afford private doctor channels. They have vast choices of consumer behaviour. These people are brand lovers, wear high-quality clothes, and eat in a cosy restaurant with quality food choices. Some of them might frequently be travelling; this group enjoys spending time on vacations. With a very smooth and convenient lifestyle, they don't avail free education. Instead of wants expensive choices in almost everything.

"THE RESILIENT ENTERPRISES"

Most Challenging 2021

- **Above the cloud:**

This class is the world's most influential people being wealthy people. People living in this category have a luxurious lifestyle among the other groups. Politicians and public figures such as actors/actresses fall under this segment. They have excessive bank funds, more fixed incomes, more investments, shares and stocks, own various businesses. Most of them own lots of properties, lots of houses, multiple vehicles, especially luxurious ones. They have the most expensive consumer behaviour. They frequently travel the world for leisure. They use private jets or go on a private flight. They take private medical facilities; perhaps some of them have their doctors and nurses. They take expensive medications, and they spend so much on education, taking their children in top rank education institutions. They give donations and sponsor charity programs to the world.

And that consists the Mevin's Consumer's Approach. The concept structured to guide you to learn more about your target customers levels and further help you understand your target customers needs and wants, and ensure to do an effective campaign to your target segment, who are most likely to purchase your product.

Vigilance – the Secret Weapon

While the use of the internet made finding out about something more efficient, we cannot always claim 100% reliability and accuracy above all. In seeking entrepreneurial opportunities through social networks, vigilance will ensure you reliable data. While this means they are just a Google away, the principle of WALK. TALK. NOTE, as discussed above, will provide you with the ideal way of gathering data of

"THE RESILIENT ENTERPRISES"
Most Challenging 2021

whatever information you need, which might help further your business. 'vigilance' merely summarizes the intelligent process WALK's TALK. NOTE concept. —everything you will learn in this concept can be simplified into one word, **"vigilance,"** needless to say, that it is indeed one of the secret weapons every resilient businessman has.

A resilient businessman doesn't only rely on information gathered virtually. While the use of the internet made all information readily available, it can't claim to be 100% accurate. We know that some of the information we get from the internet is not the same scenario in the real world. Some might be happening, most are not, we don't know. Thus, the most effective way of proving a theory is to be the one to investigate and perform it on the ground personally. – the concept of WALK. TALK.NOTE specified its process flow. We all want a reliable source, especially in business, it is but a MUST. And, the only person who could give you one is no one but yourself. Follow the concept of WALK, TALK, NOTE, and you will surely get your desired data as a reliable source in seeking entrepreneurial opportunities around, without any cloud of uncertainty on the reliability of your source. You can never go wrong with it.

"THE RESILIENT ENTERPRISES"

Most Challenging 2021

Chapter 9

"Shaping up a Business-oriented mindset."

Think of the most successful entrepreneur you know. Look back at who that person was when he was just starting. How severe were the challenges he encountered along the way? What do you think? Regardless of who that successful entrepreneur you are thinking of is, the chances are that the entrepreneur in question indeed had a success-oriented business mindset from the onset. – in doing business, various challenges come inevitably. And dealing with these ups and downs in entrepreneurship can be challenging to handle. So, to ensure success in your business endeavours and to help you maintain a mentally healthy mindset, you need to have an excellent business-oriented mindset. In this chapter, we will discuss the eight ways to help you develop an excellent business-oriented mindset. Keep going.

1. **Keep a clean and positive environment:**

When deciding to start your own business, it is imperative to have a clean and positive environment before anything else. Remember that in pursuing a business, you have to think of it critically. Thus, take time and sit back, relax, and clear up your thoughts. Attract positive energy to make up a positive environment. Your mind is the key factor. Everything has to start right there. If you wish to start up your own business and be successful with it, never skip doing this thing.

"THE RESILIENT ENTERPRISES"
Most Challenging 2021

2. Excellent imagination and visualization:

After clearing up your thoughts and free up the spaces there, that's when good vision kicks in. your mind starts visualizing concepts, good ones. As a result of clearing up everything in your mind, it will develop beneficial and powerful thoughts. Hence, our imagination is a cognitive process used in mental functioning and sometimes used in conjunction with psychological imagery. – it is considered that because it involves thinking about the possibilities. This practice, if done consistently, makes a resilient entrepreneur. And this mechanism helps you think about a wide range of possibilities and opportunities. Thus, if you ever felt like doing something new, like something different, innovative, and sophisticated, this function plays a significant role in your brain in achieving that.

3. Conceptual Thoughts:

Conceptual thinking is simply some sort of critical thinking by connecting thoughts and ideas to expand understanding, create new ideas, and reproduce from past conclusions. Conceptual thinkers can understand immaterial concepts, like the function of complex scenarios, easily. They can reinvent concepts to find more sophisticated ideas and reproduce past decisions to improve future results. This exceptional attribute is fundamental and gives people an advantage in becoming a resilient businessman.

4. Actual and virtual research:

Research is indispensably the most crucial part when starting a business is can do a fundamental analysis by putting into action the walk, talk, and note concept discussed above. You will

"THE RESILIENT ENTERPRISES"
Most Challenging 2021

personally and vigilantly observe the market's ground level and the actual market situation around you by practicing the walk talk and note guide. And, from that actual research, those results will be your initial references as your guide to study more and gather further information virtually through digital platforms, like Google, Facebook, Instagram, and Twitter. Actual research is reliable since it is your actual observation of the market. It doesn't stop right there. Reinforcing your gathered data with virtual analysis could give you more variety of references, as internet covers a broader range of information, you could get further details beyond what you can see. for example, when you develop a product especially on a specific niche, the use of actual and virtual research is essential. Both serve a significant purpose. Since when you find similar products for comparison, actual research could give you limited references only. Whereas, virtual research to find and compare similar products will provide you with various references from around the globe with multiple start-up stories you can compare and perhaps with different industries. All of which will surely give you useful information to help you shape up a good, outstanding, and resilient business-oriented mindset.

5. Hard work v. smart work:

Working smart can be said as equivalent to hard working. But working hard doesn't always really mean working smart. There's a huge difference. A resilient businessman works smart, but a typical businessman works hard. Both exert an equal amount of effort, but the results aren't always the same. working hard means spending long hours to achieve a specific goal, working smart could also mean achieving the same objective by not exhausting too much, since smart workers

"THE RESILIENT ENTERPRISES"
Most Challenging 2021

focus only on the tasks which bring them the most significant long-term impact. Simultaneously, hard workers focus more on finishing all jobs no matter what without evaluating which one impacts the business significantly and which are not. Usually, they have poor task prioritization in place. They tend to be chaotic, as they merely focus on finishing tasks that they failed to consider that the quality of completed tasks is compromised. But this isn't always the case. The discussion on which is better, working hard or working smart, is simply a talk on time-efficiency. While we still ask, work hard? Or work smart?

On the contrary, why can't we do both? Wouldn't it be more ideal? As we have discussed, resiliency is exhausting all possible resources instead of being limited between options. A resilient businessman is limitless. While working hard while working smart could be challenging to accomplish, resorting to our fast-developing technology could be of great help, time-efficiency while performing quality works intertwined more practically. We just have to go beyond the box. There are lots of ways out there. Think resiliently, work.

6. They want to get rich:

As the law of attraction suggests, we are what we always think. The universe gives us what we believe we can be. Thus, part of the process of shaping up a business-oriented mindset is to think like one. Every businessman's goal, apart from being successful, is to be rich. Hence, to be one following the principle of the law of attraction, you have to show there is a want to be rich, and the universe will help you manifest it. They want to get rich without a manifestation is just like a dream without a clear, actionable goal on how to achieve it. As such, it is likely to attract the energy of becoming one.

"THE RESILIENT ENTERPRISES"
Most Challenging 2021

7. Risk-taking ability:

Risk is not merely a risk; it is an investment instead. Taking risks leads you to so many learning impliedly, some might be something you don't expect you will learn, but since you took the risk, then you did learn unexpectedly. Not taking any risks wouldn't allow you to unveil the possibilities lying ahead. You will never know. And, only until you take risks that you will. In learning effectively, there is no such thing as spoon-feeding, indeed. To learn things that are considered your stepping stones, you have to take the steps first. One way of doing it is to take risks. Go beyond the box, as they said. A conceptual mind is better honed through learning from experiences. And, doing it by taking risks will surely give you exceptional learnings. With this, your realizations over something will be broader than that of mainstreams the typical people usually do. Be exceptional; take risks! And believe it, you will never go wrong with it. It's just you win, or you lose but with so many learnings.

8. Explore more knowledge:

Never be satisfied with the only knowledge you have. Crave for more because a resilient businessman is always hungry for learnings. Take this formula "**LEARN**" (first, we learn. Then, remove the "L" it becomes **"EARN."** Thus, the procedure goes like: learn then earn, and the cycle repeats. Which, only means, our earning is just equivalent to the knowledge we have. Hence, more learning could mean more earnings. Thus, a resilient businessman never stops learning. This applies to everyone, not only to the businessman. The more knowledge we acquire, the higher the earnings we could expect to get. And the higher is the chances of achieving goals as well. As we have mentioned, be limitless.

"THE RESILIENT ENTERPRISES"

Most Challenging 2021

The Law of Attraction

To better shape, the right business-oriented mindset, the Law of Attraction is something we should consider practising as we go on in shaping up that right mindset every resilient business person should have.

So, the Law of Attraction is a universal principle in psychology that states that "like always attracts like" – it means, if you wished for positive results, you also have to shape up your mind to entertain only the positive thoughts and attract positive outcomes. It simply means that what manifests is just the result of what we put out subconsciously. That is considered the effects of the subconscious mind's power, which explains how a person's unconscious belief affects their life ability to achieve their goals. Thus, honing your subconscious mind to send out only the right thoughts and attract more positivity is the primary key to achieving the right business-oriented mindset in a resilient way. Simply put, it's just a simple formula of wanting something. But how do you ask for it? Simple. Ask it from the universe by way of using the power of the mind. Attract what you want to manifest means, visualize where you want to see yourself heading to, as this concept believes positive thoughts attract positive outcomes, and the ball goes rolling on towards the goal.

"THE RESILIENT ENTERPRISES"

Most Challenging 2021

Chapter 10

"Another 20 years of Resilient Businesses."

F inally, in this chapter, let's discuss the upcoming trends of resilient businesses in the world.

We know that the most challenging phenomenon to predict is the future, especially that we are now in a situation where we are even struggling to figure out what's going on with today's economy and how it will get through. But, trying to predict the future is just the same as enrolling in college, starting a career afresh, or investing in new skills.

But why consider the 'future' when starting up a business?

The importance of business plans, as discussed above, answers this question.

Above all is this: keep in mind that the attribute of most successful entrepreneurs is those who don't follow the herd, but those who try to anticipate the market's needs earlier, even before the competition exists. Of course, such anticipation comes with a dose of risks, but the payout can be significant.

Be it noted that highly influential inventions such as the automobile, the internet, and smartphones are all regarded with a high degree of scepticism when first introduced. More

"THE RESILIENT ENTERPRISES"
Most Challenging 2021

importantly, the impact it retained is not only cultural but also highly economical.

For example, the automobile gave rise to a global network of small businesses such as parts makers, dealerships, and service centres, to name a few.

Also, the internet has spawned a host of online companies, Amazon.com for one, and eBay.com. Which dramatically have grown from small operations to now indeed huge ones. However, what is the small businesses of the future? Where can we find them?

The fields of energy and cleantech seem to be among the ripest areas considered to growth potential. Hence two fields of nanotechnology, entertainment, and growing demands of adapting planet to accommodate its burgeoning population, which considered even though some might strike us now as being a bit far-fetched.

Indeed, the pace of change nowadays in the world of business is a bit faster than ever. Thanks mainly to globalization and to the fast-growing digital technology. One way to spotlight the future is to stay away from those that are not.

The following are some of the businesses ideas that will be on-trend in the foreseeable future:

Data Analytics

The era of big data has started, with many firms eager to tap vast new databases to gather more information on their customer, their competitors, and even from themselves. The challenge isn't just punching numbers; in fact, it's making sense of them while gaining more useful insights that have the potential to be translated into a business edge among others.

"THE RESILIENT ENTERPRISES"

Most Challenging 2021

Marketing and market research are just two among the growing fields where the use of data is exploding. Thus, with the right gadgets and the know-how, you can easily position yourself with this time bomb business. Data is collected into a raw form for processing according to the company's requirements, which is being utilized for the company's decision-making process. This helps the company expand and grow and will give you an edge over other businesses.

With the rapid developments in our technology, data analytics is a fair business process to gain an advantage over the other, especially to close competitors. Data gathered may also be utilized to improve one's marketing efforts and advance its strategic planning, finance, and operations. Applying advanced data analytics can enable experts to come up with a more profitable and accurate decision. Data science and data analysis are the two most common terms today. Today's data is about more than just industrial oil. Data is collected in various formats, organized according to the needs of the company. This process helps companies grow and expand their business in the market, but the main question arises: What is the process's name? The answer here is data analysis. And analysts and data scientists are responsible for this process.

What is data analysis?

Data are information in the form of a guide. The proliferation of data has led to the need for data inspection to provide conclusions for analysis, data refinement, and modification and improve decision-making processes for data processing. This method is known as data analysis.

Data mining is a well-known type of data analysis technique for modelling data and retrieval of knowledge that aims to predict. Business intelligence applications provide a variety of data analytics capabilities that rely on data collection and business experience. Statistical applications can be divide into business analysis EXPLORADORES data analysis (EDA d) and confirmatory data analysis (CDA).

EDA focuses on learning new data, confirming that CDA focuses on processing existing assumptions.

Predictive analysis performs prediction or classification, focusing on statistical or structural models, while text analysis uses statistical, linguistic, and structural methods to extract and classify unstructured data from textual sources. These are all types of data analysis.

Wave information exchange has enhanced every movement in many different ways. There are many new requirements for the use of advanced analytical techniques in broad data spectra. Today, professionals can make more accurate and useful choices.

Software Engineering

Despite the vast software development being done overseas nowadays, the need for high-level computer experts capable of tying systems together is still high. In finance and investing, high-speed computing is increasingly considered a prime competitive advantage. Most companies, significantly bigger ones, will surely need networks that are way faster, more seamless, and more secured.

A Software Engineer is expected to work in a continuously evolving environment due to our rapid development of technology.

"THE RESILIENT ENTERPRISES"

Most Challenging 2021

Depending on the type of organization a software engineer works for, you might have a more distinct role within a group of IT specialists, including a system analyst, system designer, or even system tester.

Software engineers will work in a continually evolving environment due to technological advances and their strategic direction. You will create, maintain, inspect, and improve systems to meet specific needs, often recommended by a systems analyst or architect, testing hardware and software systems to diagnose and resolve system failures.

This role includes creating diagnostic programs and the design and construction of operating systems and software to improve efficiency. If necessary, we will make proposals for further development.

Functions and definitions are not uncommon in IT. Instead of being a software engineer, you could be called a programmer, engineer, or developer, depending on the system with which you are work. Alternatively, the programming language used can be part of the title, such as Java or C # merchant. The work of a program engineer can also be part of a position as a software engineer.

Depending on the company you work for, you can have a more precise role and work with a set of IT experts that can include system analysts, system designers, and system testers. However, while software engineers often manage the support systems needed to run an organization effectively, their role also allows you to communicate and effectively interpret different teams' needs to design a system.

"THE RESILIENT ENTERPRISES"

Most Challenging 2021

Space Exploring

The idea behind this future potential business is exploring and exploiting space. The reason is that the resources we have here on earth are tremendously running out. And, as foreseen, there might come a time when the value of rare metals and minerals may be worth the cost of lunar asteroid mining, especially considering that the deep-sea drilling requires an investment of about billions of dollars. If you realize that everything of value we have on earth, come to think of it are in near-infinite quantities in the space frontier. But, while others don't see it, some entrepreneurs are no longer concerned with the inherent difficulties in mining asteroids, as they are already fully convinced that these are all possible and lucrative.

Scientific Research

Foresaw Strong demand for workers who studied biology, chemistry, math, and engineering, the reason being that expected new technologies to continue generating breakthroughs in the fields of the following: medicine, manufacturing, transportation, and many other related fields. Following are the areas that show particular promise in this demand, though: biotechnology and biomedicine, nanotechnology, robotics, and 3D printings, which allows the manufacturing of physical products from a digital data file.

Bottled Air (Oxygen Canning)

"if we can water bottle water and sell, why not air?" − this potential business idea is through this ubiquitous natural resource as a product, although still at the stage of space balls. Air is undeniably more straightforward to find than a cool sip of water. In the '90s, oxygen bars went through a mildly

"THE RESILIENT ENTERPRISES"
Most Challenging 2021

popular phase. About seven or eight companies continue to market oxygen canisters to the action sports set. It carries with it the potential to increase oxygen content in our blood and can give us a boost when we're tired or fatigued. There have been no plans for pure mountain air bottles unless we try to talk about pure irony here.

Electric Car Charging Stations

In some countries, instances happen when some electric vehicles are declared completely sold even before arriving at their respective showrooms. This is how crazy the demand for electric cars is getting. Of course, that kind of demand for electric vehicles requires the same demand for electric vehicle charging stations. – this likewise addresses the concerns on the viability of buying electric cars and gives assurance that people won't hesitate to buy after worrying about how they will charge them up.

The critical point here is that these vehicles fuel up a little differently than the usual ones. Generally, these cars take hours to charge. So, stations are needed to station these cars where they can be park while charging up.

DNA Project Firms

In case you don't know, reading DNA gives clues to disease. And, at this junction in the history of human existence, DNA finally revealed some disorders. All the more if we invest in this field. But, testing DNA for patterns that are associated with diseases won't disappear so quickly. Recently, BioNaNomatrix, a Philadelphia company that provides technology solutions for reading DNA, works on a grant to get DNA sequencing under $100 by 2020. The foreseen long-term opportunities for more

"THE RESILIENT ENTERPRISES"
Most Challenging 2021

affordable DNA testing include a better understanding of ageing and the endless possibilities for new ways to treat and cure disease. The envisioned chance of making this work is first to take a person's DNA when they are still a baby, take a profile of it in a systematic process, and predict the baby's health status more efficiently and organized.

Nanosatellite

The idea behind this is not only about making things smaller than it was half a century ago, but it also aimed at pursuing a lower cost of launching them. Can be inserted Nanosatellites and picosatellites with all sorts of useful equipment that have business applications. The types of nanosatellites and microsatellites built by small companies and universities; therefore in future will become more robust. Needless to point out that this indeed pushes us on the verge where small teams and companies will be able to be efficient from a smaller package. Therefore when technology enhancing the business climate always concerning about useability and efficiency.

Robotics Engineers

With the damage caused by the improvised explosive device in Iraq and Iran to thousands of robots, the need for robot mechanics lies. They are already existing.

Right now, some companies are already engaging robots in doing some tasks. These robots are scrubbing the floors, but they cannot wash dishes. What we envision as a potential business is the ubiquitous one, just like a computer repair shop.

Recently, the world robot population's growth was wild, with an estimated 13 million robots, according to IFR World Robotics. Many of these are industrial robots, but personal robotics is also multiplying, with a vision of producing ones capable of doing dishes and ironing. Such a growing trend means the same level of demand for robotics engineers. And, those soldiers who risk their lives trying to save robots on the battlefields are expect to accelerate massively too.

Greenhouse Farming

Do you know that high-tech greenhouses save significant amounts of water and increase productivity? – so, why don't we stack them up and make cities self-efficient? This idea of vertical farms came from an infectious disease ecologist, Dickson Despommier, who turned his knowledge of parasites into foreseeing cities.

"Instead for the city to behave like a parasite, it should be a symbiont. He said the future city has to take a big lesson from nature and start acting like an ecosystem. By saying that, he means zero-waste cities.

Greenhouse's advantages are as follows: fair distribution of light inside the greenhouse occurs apart from excellent ventilation.

Greenhouse cultivation refers to growth structures (wood, plastic, metal, and mesh) and cultivation in controlled environments. Greenhouses protect crops from adverse weather conditions, pests, and diseases and offer high-quality products, high prices, and higher yields.

1. Fresh vegetables, fruits, and vegetables.

2. Availability and success of the transplant.

3. Fresh flowers throughout the year.

"THE RESILIENT ENTERPRISES"

Most Challenging 2021

4. A warm place to visit in the middle of winter, grey winters.

5. The ability to grow things that you would not otherwise be able to grow (exotic flowers, tropical fruits)

The main advantages of the greenhouse are the direct distribution of light in the greenhouse. The greenhouse cover can deflect the sun's rays, so it is evenly distributed over the entire surface, benefits the greenhouse, and protects plants from direct sunlight. Energy efficiency. It makes better use of environmental conditions, such as generating heat in a greenhouse. Microclimate control. One of the main benefits of a greenhouse is that it controls and establish the ideal environment for cultivation. Can Temperature be adjusted, humidity, lighting, etc.? Protection against diseases, pests, and other insects. Another benefit of the greenhouse is that it is tough to enter, as it is an enclosed space with excellent ventilation. You can quickly ventilate greenhouses thanks to zenithal or side windows. The strongest line against rain and wind. Production increases production. This is an excellent advantage of a greenhouse, increasing productivity due to weather conditions, speeding up plants' growth, and allowing more plant periodic production. Can produce the greenhouse from time to time to better selling price and continuous product production in unfavourable weather conditions. Weight loss, followed by fatigue, and constant tiredness can receive more than one annual crop and various plants. Optimizes the use of other technologies to support climate control (heating, humidity, shade insulation or energy saving, etc.)

"THE RESILIENT ENTERPRISES"

Most Challenging 2021

Mobile Marketing Consulting

The increase in the number of people who surf the web using mobile devices like smartphones and tablets paved the way to consider adopting mobile device marketing to target prospects that use mobile devices, which likewise resulted in the formation of that high demand for mobile marketing consultants. Also, because indicators suggest that mobile devices will continue to dominate for a more extended period, with the need for mobile marketing, the potential opportunity for mobile marketing consultants will soon be on the rise.

Social Media Consulting

The rise in social networking sites like Facebook, Instagram, and Twitter, made it necessary for businesses to consider using these platforms when reaching out to prospects. These resulted in a massive demand for marketing consultants who advise companies on promoting and marketing their products and services on social networks. And, such demand will continue increasing for as long as social media continues to remain significant.

A social media consultant will be your guide to successfully reach your audience and develop an effective social media marketing campaign. A social media consultant will help you reach your audience and use relevant social media campaigns to drive traffic to your website.

This must be a workable process and technique because, in the future, no one will start a business without social media; no one will be able to raise awareness by skipping this process. So, social media consultation is essential for jobs and companies. A business should always update with trends and changes continuously. Knowledge is vital to living as a resilient entrepreneur.

Business Process Outsourcing

As a result of this swift twist in the standard economy's situation, businesses have to digitize. They are constrained to find efficient ways to cut down their cost and streamline their operations. One way of achieving it is by outsourcing to freelance contractors on positions that used to be in-house functions, such as, accounting, human resources and IT-related tasks. Thus, if you could set up a competitive outsourcing agency with competent people, you are in for substantial potential profit.

Can define Business process outsourcing as the process of contracting specific work processes to an external service provider such as accounting, telemarketing, data recording, social media marketing, customer support, and many more.

What Is Business Process Outsourcing?

Business process outsourcing (BPO) is the process of contracting one or more specific work to an external service provider, including payroll, accounting, telemarketing, data logging, social media marketing, customer support, and more. BPOs typically cater to business development functions - other core services - which can be technical or non-technical.

From new beginnings to large Fortune 500 companies, businesses of all sizes are outsourcing, and demand is growing. New and innovative jobs are creating, and businesses are looking for the best way forward. BPO can be another way of migrating workers, allowing workers to remain in their own country, providing their experience abroad.

"THE RESILIENT ENTERPRISES"

Most Challenging 2021

The BPO is divide into two main types of services: back office and front office. Back-office services include internal business practices, such as billing or purchase. Forward-office services related to the clients of a compliant company, such as marketing and support tech BPOs can combine these services so they can work together.

The BPO business is divide into three categories, based on the location of the seller. A company can achieve strategic planning by combining three components:

Offshore vendors are outside the company's country. For example, an Australian company could use an offshore BPO dealer in Sri Lanka.

Nearshore vendors are located in countries adjacent to the company with which contract was contracted. For example, in Australia, a public service provider in Indonesia is considered a short-shore provider.

Onshore vendors work locally with the contractor, although they may be in a different city or state. For example, a base company, Melbourne Australia, could use an existing coastal retailer, Adelaide, or Hobart, Australia

Web Designing

As the digital age came in, every small to large businesses have gradually started to establish their online presence through websites, paving the way for web designers to rise enormously. Starting a business in web design is more economical, especially considering that the situation we are currently in made it difficult for us to start up a business with enough capital. It isn't the case in starting your own business in web designing, though. Because, with a PC, a good internet connection, and an amount of creativity, you are on the go if you wish to pursue this field. Thus, if you are excellently skilled in the field of technology or have completed your study in computer science, this is the ideal business start-up for you.

Having an online presence isn't optional for businesses nowadays, considering the technological advancement these times. Thus, a business website becomes the first place your prospects might interact to know about your brand. As such, it is a must that your website exceeds your customer's expectations, and if possible, it should contain every detail you need to let your customers know about who you are and a clear message of what you can do.

Having an online presence isn't optional for businesses nowadays, considering the technological advancement these times. Thus, a business website becomes the first place your prospects might interact to know about your brand. As such, it is a must that your website exceeds your customer's expectations, and if possible, it should contain every detail you need to let your customers know about who you are and a clear message of what you can do.

Online presence is no longer an option for your company. B2C and B2B website customers use the internet to get answers to their questions. Your website is always the first place a new prospect engages with your brand. In fact, after the page loads, you'll have 0.05 seconds to impress your visitor, and 94% of people cited web design as a reason to distrust or rejected a website. As a business owner, it is more important for your website to exceed what customers expect and provide clear and concrete information about who you are and what you can do.

So what makes a good website different?. Of course, some design rules can be highlighted or even some examples of today's design trends. The truth is that design is subjective. What looks great to one person seems terrible to another. In addition to this challenge, a report from Adobe states that "two-thirds want to read something more beautifully designed than normal because they are giving 15 minutes to consume content." there is.

Search Engine Optimization (SEO)

What is SEO?

SEO means search engine optimization, which is the process of increasing the amount of traffic to your website through organic search results.

How Does SEO WORK?

You can think of a search engine as a website that you visit to type (or discuss) a question box. Google, Yahoo!, Bing, or whatever search engine you use, magically responds to a long list of website links that might answer your question.

It's true. But have you ever wondered what's behind these magical link lists?

Here's how it works: Google (or whatever search engine you use) has a crawler. Collects information about anything they can find on the internet. Crawlers return all 1s and 0s to the search engine to create an index. That index is then through an algorithm that tries to match all the data to your query. Again, the demand for good SEO services is relatively increasing because of the situation we currently have. This service is related to web designing. This exists on every webmaster who

"THE RESILIENT ENTERPRISES"
Most Challenging 2021

owns a website to be detected by search engines and people to increase their profit margin. The good thing about it is you can provide SEO services from the comforts of your home. To survive the competition, though, make sure that your learning curve will not stop anytime soon. Make sure to equip yourself with every new search engine update and improve and change your SEO tactics regularly to survive the field's competition. Meaning, consistent research is an investment for you.

Accounting organizations

You can start your small accounting firm without a strong economic and financial background for accountants. You are on the go with just your professional degree and, of course, practical and competitive accounting knowledge.

The truth is, regardless of the business, everyone requires an accountant. If you are an accountant, consider starting your accounting firm now. Just give your best, irrespective of the size – small, medium, or large scale. Give the best you can offer for your client's benefit. Because, nowadays, satisfied clients are the best advertisements you could have for your business. And, with this, your business will indeed survive the competition.

"THE RESILIENT ENTERPRISES"

Most Challenging 2021

Management organizations

The management firm's primary objective in an organization is to tell people who work for the organization what they should do, when, and to ensure they can.

Therefore, management must take care of the team in all types of functions that serve the organization, such as business strategy, hiring, accounting, investment, law, research, methodology, recruitment, security, administration, public relations, shareholder relations, as well as the fundamental functions of selling the company's products or services and delivering them following the agreed terms of the contract

Many companies have different types of pain points in their organizations. Management consultants or companies can present their real requirements and maximize the end goal.

The boss earns a lot for one good reason: his job isn't as easy as it might seem. The future suggests that effective management shall require primary business knowledge and the ability to oversee operations in so many locations and countries, and some necessary know-how. So, the demand for anybody who can improve a unit's performance while lowering costs is foreseeing to rise. The BLS and IBIS World are also expecting a growth in demand for support fields like human relations, benefits administration, and event planning.

A management firm's primary purpose is to look after staff, give command of what they need to do when to do it, and ensure that they can do it.

"THE RESILIENT ENTERPRISES"

Most Challenging 2021

Freelance Workers' Marketplace

People like to work with a free mind and with fewer commitments, but you must also follow the organization's guidelines when working for a company. Still, if you plan to start a self-employed business now, there are many online platforms to improve. If you think you have a talent or passion for some professional job, you now have a potential market open. And you don't have to worry about where you are, what time you work, it just depends on your capacity and dedication.

COVID-19 indeed made a sudden shift towards digitization, which caused all the companies to engage freelancers and contract workers to fill their staff's skill gaps. According to Freelancer.com, which lists more than a million freelance projects on its site, the most in-demand freelance services currently are data entry, academic writing, excel projects, data processing, web search, and Facebook-based jobs. Accordingly, some freelance gigs are being paid by the project, while some get paid hourly, and the rates vary. But the sure thing is, as you gain more experience, the higher your potential income becomes.

Bio-Fuel Manufacturing

Biofuels are fuels produced directly or indirectly from organic matter - biomass - including plants and animal waste.

In total, bioenergy covers about 10% of the world's total energy demand. Traditional raw plants such as wood, charcoal, and animal dung cause many of these and are the primary source of energy for most people in developing countries, who are used to cooking and heating.

"THE RESILIENT ENTERPRISES"
Most Challenging 2021

More sophisticated and efficient conversion technologies have made it possible to extract biofuels from materials such as wood, crops, and waste. Biofuels can be reliable, gaseous, or liquid, although the term is often used in the literature in a narrow way to refer to liquid biofuels only for transportation.

Can derive Biofuels from crops, including conventional food plants or particular energy crops. Can also obtain Biofuels from forestry, agricultural and marine products, household waste, agriculture, food industry, food service by-products, and waste.

There are different forms of bio-fuels with various sources, too, which are most cost-effective. Fuel is likewise cheap, not to mention that it can make it from waste. And the most crucial factor to consider is that biofuels don't emit smoke as the conventional energy sources do—the kerosene, petrol and, all the like we have around here. You can start producing your bio-fuel and create your invention that would run on bio-fuel, perhaps like a generator, a bicycle, or a motor vehicle, maybe.

Electric Cars Manufacturing

A battery electric vehicle or BEV uses electricity stored in a battery pack to power an electric motor and spin its wheels.

When depleted, the battery is recharged using grid electricity from a wall outlet or a dedicated charging device. Battery electric vehicles and trucks are considered "electric" cars because they are not powered by gasoline or diesel but are powered entirely by electricity.

When driving, BEVs do not cause exhaust pipe contamination, and there are no exhaust pipes. However, the electricity they use can cause heat-trapping gases and other pollution from the

"THE RESILIENT ENTERPRISES"
Most Challenging 2021

source or fossil fuel extraction. The amount of pollution produced depends on how the electricity is being made. In the United States, battery-electric cars charged from the dirtiest coal-dominated grid still generate less pollution than their petrol-powered counterparts. BEVs are removed from sources such as air or sun.

Expenditures on fuel are one huge burden everyone, especially those with vehicles, carries daily. − I can only imagine how happy these people will lessen this burden. Just imagine a world where you don't have to fuel your vehicle. With this idea in mind, you can develop your electric vehicle or perhaps employ people to develop one and sell the idea to you for reproduction. There is undeniably a vast potential market waiting for this, for sure. − people will indeed embrace this innovation with their arms wide open. However, one huge factor to consider is having a wealthy pocket when planning to do this kind of business. And, doubts might be lingering around you on whether or not cars can run on electricity. The answer is yes! If you could do a little bit of research, will indeed clear clouds on your mind.

In a world full of uncertainty, resiliency is a MUST for an entrepreneur to survive in the business world. Not only will it save you from the darkness of the unknown, but it will also prepare you to combat the constantly changing market where only those who can effectively foresee what lies ahead can step their business forward. If you do not know, find out more about being a resilient businessman. Learn more about how resilient a business person should be to reign over the challenges the world is randomly giving, like this catastrophic pandemic from which we are all suffering and struggling.

"THE RESILIENT ENTERPRISES"
Most Challenging 2021

In this world, the only constant is "change". – Which is a considerable challenge in the world of business. One notable event is the world-altering outbreak of the COVID-19, which significantly made a significant impact in all industries all over the globe, with no exemptions. With this business climate, the world is experiencing, what future awaits every business person in 2021? Will there still be businessmen with brave hearts to take some risks all over again? Which enterprise can we consider starting up in the COVID aftermath? – Ever wonder what it takes to be a resilient businessman? Congratulations! You're on your way to finding out after reading this book. This book will teach you the qualities a resilient entrepreneur should have to survive this journey towards the unknown.

It is crucial that before you decide to take the path of entrepreneurship, conceptual imagination is the first thing you know, and when it's come to the commercial level of how the system of the business works. Make sure to fully equip yourself with what is necessary, especially now that industry is becoming riskier as different generations pass.

"THE RESILIENT ENTERPRISES"

Most Challenging 2021

Research / Observations / conclusions / citations and related theories

articles.bplans.com – Mr Parsons – Business Planning | blue16media.com – Digital Platforms | investopedia.com – organisations floor | thehartford.com – Business insurance | gstregister.com – Tax | coschedule.com – Social media platforms | talkingtalent.prosky.co – employee grooming | marketing.pinecc.com – Important of Technology | cgsinc.com – in-house matters of technology | ama.org – Marketing practise | bionity.com – Nanomatrix | smartsheet.com – BPO Operations | smamarketing.net – website appearance | moz.com – search engine optimisation | auessays.com – Management factors | greenfacts.org – biofuel | ucsusa.org – electric cars and batteries | acciona.com – wind energy | greenmatch.co. – Energy source | investopedia.com – business consultations | entrepreneur.com – psychology factors | indeed.com – career development | smallbusinessconnections.com.au – business | profitableventure.com – data analytics | seek.com – employments | Wikipedia – general knowledge

www.ingramcontent.com/pod-product-compliance
Lightning Source LLC
Chambersburg PA
CBHW072030230526
45466CB00020B/1204